PUTTING DOWN ROOTS

PUTTING DOWN ROOTS

Gardening Insights from Wisconsin's Early Settlers

Marcia C. Carmichael

WISCONSIN HISTORICAL SOCIETY PRESS

Published by the Wisconsin Historical Society Press
Publishers since 1855

wisconsinhistory.org

Frontmatter photo credits: Page ii, Old World Wisconsin's James and Rebecca Sanford Farm kitchen garden, Mike Morbeck; page vii, *The Ladies' Floral Cabinet and Pictorial Home Companion* 3, 1874; pages viii-ix, planting the garden at the Friedrich and Sophia Koepsell Farm restoration, Mike Morbeck; page x, interpreter using a long-spouted watering-pot at the Wesley and Sophia Benson House garden, Mike Morbeck; page xiv, historical gardeners weeding in the Sanford garden, Terry Molter.

Photographs identified with WHi or WHS are from the Society's collections; address requests to reproduce these photos to the Visual Materials Archivist at the Wisconsin Historical Society, 816 State Street, Madison, WI 53706.

Printed in Canada
Designed by Steve Biel

15 14 13 12 11   1 2 3 4 5

Library of Congress Cataloging-in-Publication Data

Carmichael, Marcia C.
Putting down roots : gardening insights from Wisconsin's early settlers / Marcia C. Carmichael.
p. cm.
Includes bibliographical references and index.
ISBN 978-0-87020-466-1 (pbk. : alk. paper) 1. Gardens—Wisconsin—History. 2. Old World Wisconsin (Museum) I. Title. II. Title: Gardening insights from Wisconsin's early settlers.
SB451.34.W6C37 2011
635.09775—dc22
2010043324

∞ The paper used in this publication meets the minimum requirements of the American National Standard for Information Sciences—Permanence of Paper for Printed Library Materials, ANSI Z39.48-1992.

Publication of this book was made possible in part by a major gift from the Kettle Moraine Garden Club. Additional funding was provided by the Herb Society of America–Wisconsin Unit, the Maihaugen Foundation, the Will Ross Memorial Foundation, and an anonymous donor.

For the dedicated Old World Wisconsin
staff and volunteers

Contents

Acknowledgments

As holds true with all ambitious projects, many wonderful people offered their knowledge, talents, time, and support as I researched and wrote this book. The following people assisted me immensely—above and beyond my expectations. I am very grateful to them and to many, many others who generously provided information and insight.

The fabulous Old World Wisconsin staff has been extremely kind and helpful. They pitched in when needed so that I might retain some semblance of sanity as I tried to balance work and book.

Ellen Penwell, curator of collections at Old World Wisconsin, has done extensive research on the history of garden tools and furnishes the site's historical gardeners with usable appropriate tools—many reproduced from originals, and others created from illustrations and descriptions in nineteenth-century gardening manuals. Ellen graciously shares her expertise on historical garden tools in the sidebar narratives she contributed throughout this book.

Marty Perkins, Old World Wisconsin's curator of research, has served as this book's in-house editor and valued advisor. He generously shared volumes from his personal library and patiently answered question after question from this struggling author. Marty has been part of Old World Wisconsin since its inception and, fortunately for me, has a remarkably fine memory. His advice, perspective, and support have been invaluable.

Jennifer Van Haaften, curator of interpretation at Old World Wisconsin, kindly reviewed historical recipes chosen for the book and was very helpful in translating them for modern usage.

The in-depth studies of German and Polish settlers in Wisconsin, prepared for Old World Wisconsin by Jim Miller and Susan Mikos respectively, provided well-researched documentation, for which I am extremely grateful.

Photographers Gerry and Signe Emmerich, Nancy Klemp, Sandy Matson, and Terry Molter very generously donated their time and talents to photograph the plants and gardens at Old World Wisconsin—often on a moment's notice. Their creative work delivered outstanding examples of their dedication to perfection.

Loyd Heath, Mike Morbeck, and Larry Dickerson also generously shared their wonderful photographs, rounding out the fine images of the re-created gardens.

In addition to offering her photographic skills, Sandy Matson coordinated photographers' visits, compiled images, and spent countless hours poring through and organizing pictures. She also stepped in as occasional research assistant—tracking down information by computer, phone, and trips to libraries—and back-up typist.

Deb Balis magically transformed pages and pages of handwritten ink scratchings into an electronically transferable manuscript. She kindly made herself available at unusual times, any day of the week, so that I could continue my full-time job and still make book deadlines.

The supportive staff of the Old World Wisconsin Foundation originally suggested I put together a small garden booklet. Periodically they delivered meals so that my husband would have something to eat while this book totally consumed me.

Laura Kearney, my Wisconsin Historical Society Press editor, was very kind and encouraging throughout this undertaking and—to my delight—shares my enthusiasm for plants. I greatly appreciated her attention to detail along every step in the process of this book's creation.

My wonderful husband patiently—or resignedly—tolerated life with an overloaded historical gardener/writer during this project. He deserves a medal (though he would rather have a tractor).

My parents have always given me their loving encouragement to pursue my dreams. Their support never wavered through this endeavor.

This book could never have been written without the Old World Wisconsin historical garden volunteers. They turn my plans and visions for the gardens into reality. In addition to their hard work through long hours, they supplied encouragement, humor, and numerous welcome desserts. They brighten my days and always amaze me with their dedication and generosity.

I am very fortunate to have had the kindness and support of all these—and many more—incredible people. This book has truly been a labor of love.

Introduction

Wisconsin might seem an unlikely destination for emigrants from a multitude of countries in the nineteenth century. But when its attributes are considered, it is easy to imagine the promise and the excitement of those packing their trunks, daring to dream of a new home and a chance at a better life.

The immigrants collected provisions for the journey, carefully selected items deemed necessary to begin life in the New World, and gathered treasured possessions and mementos from home. Housewives felt pride and wariness as they carefully packed seeds, roots, and slips of plants to grow and nourish their families. Vegetables for food, herbs for healing, and flowers for the soul—all would be vital to making life bearable in the unfamiliar country.

Whether leaving their homeland because of economic, political, religious, or social hardships or answering the call to explore new lands and greater opportunities, these immigrants seized the chance to exert some control over their futures. Old World Wisconsin's curator of research Martin Perkins describes the pattern of early migration into the state: "The immigrants poured out of Europe into Wisconsin. Initially, they journeyed from places like England, Ireland, and Scotland. By the late 1830s Pomeranian settlers from the Baltic coast joined those from the British Isles. Scandinavian influences soon blended into the state's ethnic mosaic with the arrival of home-seekers from Norway, Denmark, and Sweden. This contagious immigration fever eventually spread throughout central, southern, and eastern Europe. By the late nineteenth century, it brought countless others, such as Bohemian, Polish, and Finnish families, who further enhanced the Badger State's cultural fabric."[1]

Wisconsin offered affordable land, rich soil, access to fine waterways and transportation routes, abundant timber and wild game, and a climate similar to the homelands left behind—if the glowing reports could be believed. Promotional materials published by land agents as well as by the state and private industry provided enthusiastic descriptions and welcoming invitations. Opportunities abounded! Earlier settlers wrote letters home, encouraging family members, friends, and neighbors to join them in the

new country. Here at last they could own land, shape their destinies, reap the rewards of their hard work, and ensure a brighter future for their children. In Wisconsin, all things were possible!

The earliest pioneers hunted, fished, and foraged for food. When settled, they planted basic reliable crops that grew readily and could be stored for winter sustenance, for survival. Root crops fulfilled the requirements. Initially ground was broken by hand or with the aid of oxen. Fences enclosed the gardens to discourage roaming farm livestock and wild animals. The immigrants found comfort in growing familiar plants and added favorites when they could. More than one treasured rose endured the arduous ocean voyage and challenging journey overland by ox-drawn covered wagon, nestled snugly in a basket or iron kettle.[2] Precious seeds and plant material brought from the Old Country quickly went into the ground and received careful nurturing. Seeds or tubers of the best specimens often were collected and saved for the next season's crop. Letters written home frequently carried requests for additional seeds or plant material. New World neighbors shared and traded with one another. Sometimes seeds and plants could be purchased from traveling salesmen, local vendors, or nurseries. When the railroad crossed the state, mail order became big business. Numerous seed companies published successful catalogs advertising vegetable, flower, and herb seeds for sale. Enterprising seedsman James Vick, who had established a thriving business based in Rochester, New York, issued catalogs in multiple languages in order to serve—and profit from—European immigrants in America.

As the people prospered, their houses, surroundings, and quality of life improved. Interior spaces received attention, and ladies took particular interest in dressing up their front rooms or parlors. Plants played a key role in creating the desired decorative effect. For some families the embellishment continued outdoors with landscape enhancement.

Old World Wisconsin, the largest of the Wisconsin Historical Society's living history museums, traces the development of different immigrant populations in the nineteenth-century Wisconsin environment. Since its inception in the 1970s, the museum has collected historic buildings from around the state, relocated them, and painstakingly restored them on a site carefully laid out over 576 acres in Eagle, Waukesha County. Numerous farmsteads and a crossroads village showcase rural life. Re-created, historically accurate gardens complement the settings of a dozen homes from various ethnic backgrounds and delight the senses of visitors.

Situated within a large, historically appropriate natural setting with diverse topography, the re-created farm and village landscapes and the numerous gardens representing a wide variety of ethnicities—all based on extensive studies of historical sources—make Old World Wisconsin unique among living history museums. The carefully researched gardens filled with vegetables, flowers, herbs, and fruits of varying colors, textures, flavors, and

NINETEENTH-CENTURY GARDEN WRITERS

Numerous nineteenth-century garden writers shared valuable information. Some favorites wrote with a sense of humor or with passion and compassion for plants and fellow gardeners.

In his 1863 gardening classic *The Field and Garden Vegetables of America*, Fearing Burr Jr. accurately but charitably described dandelions as "spontaneously abundant" and then went on to devote two pages to their preferred culture and usage![1]

Mrs. S. O. Johnson, aka "Daisy Eyebright"—obviously directing her 1870s writings to a Yankee readership in her charming book *Every Woman Her Own Flower Gardener*—took women by the hand and gently encouraged and instructed them to step into the garden themselves and experience the delights of exercise firsthand.

The "thoroughly amiable"[2] James Vick, a brilliant marketer, successful seedsman, and editor, wrote in a comfortable style with love and enthusiasm for plants and gardens and with kindness and patience for the readers of his magazines and catalogs. In an 1878 issue of his popular *Vick's Illustrated Monthly Magazine*, the words he used to describe the lessons that can be learned from the culture of flowers could easily be applied to the nineteenth-century practice of planting and gardening in general: "It teaches industry, patience, faith, and hope. We plant and sow in hope, and patiently wait with faith in the rainbow promise that harvest shall never fail."[3]

A circa 1880 cover of an issue of *Vick's Flower and Vegetable Garden*

NOTES

1. Fearing Burr Jr., *The Field and Garden Vegetables of America* (Boston: Crosby and Nichols, 1863), 345.

2. L. H. Bailey, *Cyclopedia of American Horticulture*, vol. 4 (New York: The MacMillan Company, 1903), 1928.

3. *Vick's Illustrated Monthly Magazine* (Rochester, NY: James Vick, February 1878), 33–34.

fragrances are planted and maintained by Old World Wisconsin historical garden staff and volunteers. Research is ongoing, and the gardens continue to evolve as additional information comes to light. They accurately represent the time period and the ethnicity of the exhibits they complement, such as the kitchen garden appropriate for an 1860 German immigrant's farm where plants—from marshmallow to mignonette, rutabagas to roses, and summer savory to scorzonera—transform the entire front yard into a well-ordered patchwork quilt design.

Some deep digging has been necessary to unearth descriptions of the plants and gardens grown by nineteenth-century Wisconsin settlers. Because the gardens of the wealthy or the elite were much more frequently captured in words and art than were the plantings of common folk, our search for information takes numerous paths. Voices of the nineteenth century speak from letters and diaries in which personal observations, experiences, and emotions are shared. Nineteenth-century newspapers, magazines, and transactions of state horticultural and agricultural societies offer valuable insights into planting trends and practices, popular plant varieties, and challenges faced in gardening and farming. Books and seed catalogs of the period provide tremendous amounts of information. Recipes and cookbooks of each ethnic population shed light on popular plants for kitchen use, favorite flavors, and preferred methods of preparation. Nineteenth-century illustrations and photographs are often amazing or delightful—and always educational.

Public records, including census information, estate probates, and life lease agreements are also consulted in the compilation of this ethnic garden information. Old World Wisconsin's research files provide documented interviews with relatives, descendants, and neighbors of many of the families whose homes now reside on the historic site's grounds and whose re-created gardens are described in the following pages. Research reports and unpublished manuscripts prepared for Old World Wisconsin over several decades offer a wealth of information. Numerous secondary sources are extremely valuable; many of the works consulted for this book are listed in the selected bibliography. Online searches are also conducted, and we tap into the Wisconsin branches of the cultural and historical societies of many different ethnic groups. Through the use of previously uncompiled sources related to nineteenth-century settlers' gardens we hope to advance scholarship on this fascinating subject—and perhaps inspire you to look to your own roots.

With the current interest in treating the environment gently, gardening organically, and eating locally grown food, many people are looking back to the gardening practices of previous generations. Much of the advice directed to gardeners in the nineteenth century has changed little over the years and may be recognized as relevant and timeless. Well over a century later, garden experts continue to recommend the rotation of crops, to work toward soil improvement, and to fight many of the same pests and weeds.

Even old tools become new again as the modern gardener discovers that laborsaving devices need not involve noisy, noxious, fume-producing engines. It is interesting to re-examine some of the tools that were available in the second half of the nineteenth century. Curator of collections at Old World Wisconsin Ellen Penwell has contributed many of the sidebar narratives scattered throughout the following pages, providing information on a number of garden-related objects.

Readers looking to connect with their own family's gardening heritage may find inspiration in this book. We explore gardening practices, styles, and trends of early Yankee arrivals as well as those of Irish, German, Polish, Norwegian, Finnish, and Danish immigrants—just a sampling of Wisconsin's rich ethnic settlement. In addition, you will find listings of plants commonly grown in the kitchen gardens of these nineteenth-century immigrants who brought their traditional plants, foods, and recipes when they settled in Wisconsin, as well as a sampling of historical recipes to capture the flavors of the harvest. For the most part the selected recipes have been copied directly from original sources, complete with unusual spellings and punctuation, allowing their nineteenth-century charm to shine through. Explanations have been added as needed for clarification or to provide additional information.

Twenty-first-century gardeners are fortunate to have access to seeds and plant material from around the world, making it possible to create their own ethnic gardens filled with heirloom plants. Savor the tasty difference authentic ingredients can make in the kitchen as you prepare recipes with historical varieties of vegetables, fruits, and herbs. Or treat yourself to some of the fragrant flowers and herbs early settlers grew. Select your favorite plants, seeds, and recipes and share them with your family and friends. As you continue the tradition of passing along these heirlooms, you will experience the joys these garden treasures have brought to people for generations.

YANKEE SETTLER GARDENS

1

Looking Forward to a Brighter Future

The wilds of Wisconsin were forever changed with the arrival of the Yankees in ever-increasing numbers from the mid-1830s through the 1860s. These American-born settlers of British ancestry came from the northeastern states, leaving crowded living conditions and exhausted farmland behind, to settle in southeastern Wisconsin. There they found rich prairie soil, fine oak trees to provide building material as well as fuel, and good water from nearby lakes.

Well educated and well read, the Yankees sought to bring civilization to the wilderness. Convinced of their moral and intellectual superiority, many showed great interest in establishing, improving, and influencing local schools, churches, and government. The newly arrived settlers erected simple log or primitive frame homes and planted strictly utilitarian gardens to ensure the family's survival. As the people prospered, they built finer homes, usually frame or brick, and found much advice available on the subjects of agriculture and gardening in numerous new and popular publications.

Authors recommended the ideal garden be situated on level ground, preferably with a gentle slope toward the south or southeast. They advised protection from northerly winds and stressed the importance of well-drained soil: ideally friable, loamy, and trenched to a depth of eighteen inches. "But never let a clay or driving sand even, deter you from the good work, as the former is easily subdued by draining, thorough exposure to the frosts of winter . . . and applying all light loosening materials that can be got at, as coal ashes, sand, road or street sweepings, refuse from the woods, and similar material. Blowing sands are also to be improved by the opposite practice," a writer suggested in an 1858 periodical article titled "The Kitchen Garden."[1]

The kitchen garden included plants necessary for the care and feeding of the household. Often described as the area in which vegetables, herbs, and small fruits were

Previous spread:
The James and Rebecca Sanford Farm at Old World Wisconsin, a re-created Wisconsin Yankee kitchen garden, circa 1860
GERALD H. EMMERICH JR.

Opposite page:
A few neatly laid-out straight main paths allow easy access to the kitchen garden.
GERALD H. EMMERICH JR.

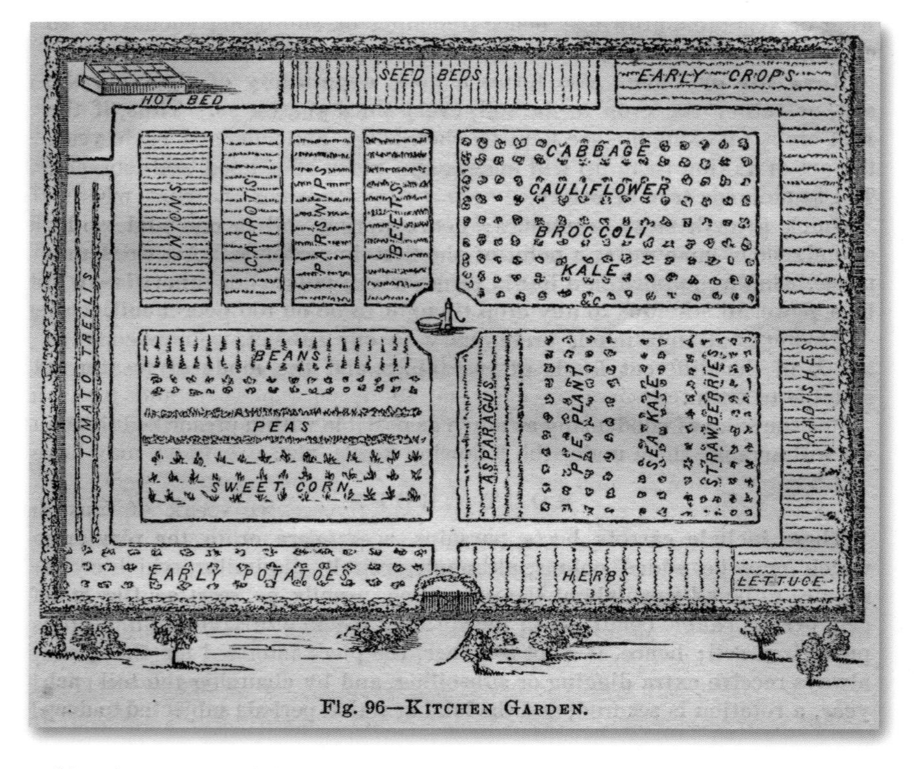

A line drawing of a kitchen garden recommended in an 1858 periodical.
EDGAR SANDERS, "THE KITCHEN GARDEN," *THE ILLUSTRATED ANNUAL REGISTER OF RURAL AFFAIRS FOR 1858*, NO. 4

grown "for the supply of the table,"[2] this garden also grew ingredients for household medicines, fragrant products, insect repellents, and dyes for yarn and cloth. With the garden laid out in a square or rectangular shape, a fence (up to six feet or higher!) or a strong, dense, and frequently prickly hedge enclosed the plantings, protecting them from damaging winds as well as from outside intruders—both four- and two-legged. Any standard trees were planted outside the fence, far enough away to prevent potential damage to garden plants by thirsty and invasive tree roots, shading leaves, or droppings that might injure the vegetation below.

A straight main path, three to six feet wide, typically ran through the center of the garden, and a second path often bisected the first, dividing the garden into quadrants. Within the quadrants, crops were planted in beds separated by narrower paths or in rows. Entire beds devoted to beets, carrots, turnips, parsnips, and onions ensured a year's supply for the family. Other vegetables, commonly laid out in rows, included bush and pole beans, peas, cabbage, and, in lesser quantities, cauliflower, broccoli, salsify (or vegetable oyster), radishes, and celery. The more cold-sensitive tomatoes (or love apples), eggplant, and peppers received an early start in hotbeds. The vining crops of cucumbers, summer and winter squash, and melons filled sizable areas designated for

THE GARDEN MARKER AND LINE REEL

Nineteenth-century garden manuals typically included a chapter on recommended gardening tools; these books are an indispensable resource to the modern researcher. Many of the tools described and illustrated, such as garden hoes and watering-pots, were available only by purchase. The books also discussed innovative plans for implements that ingenious and thrifty gardeners might make themselves. The multitoothed garden marker was such a tool, easily made from materials found on the farm.

The garden marker efficiently drew up to six lines, or rows, in the soil in preparation for seeding. For large garden beds the garden marker was preferred over the line reel. Comprised of a metal stake with a revolving spool of twine, the line reel guided the seeding of single rows, one by one.

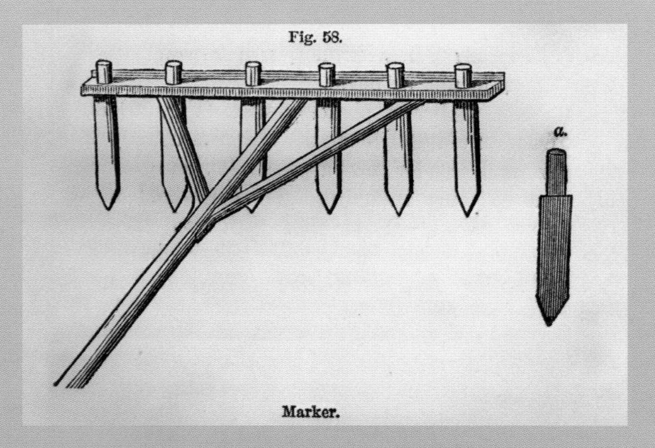

The garden marker, illustrated in Alexander Watson's *The American Home Garden*, 1859

A reproduction garden marker in use at Old World Wisconsin
NANCY L. KLEMP

THE GARDEN MARKER AND LINE REEL

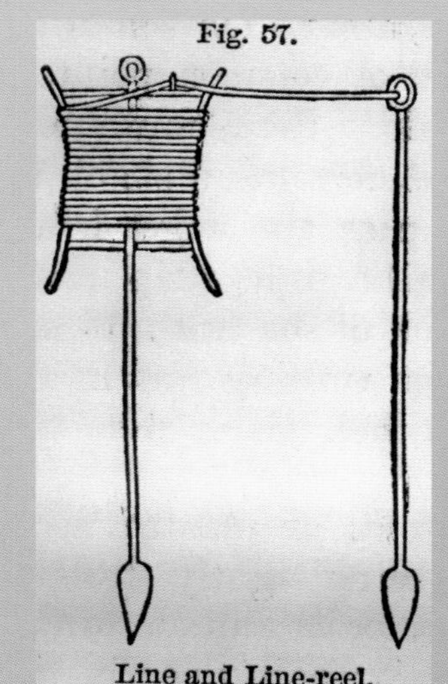

An illustration of the line reel in *The American Home Garden*, 1859

A line reel
NANCY L. KLEMP

In the 1859 garden manual *The American Home Garden*, Alexander Watson describes how a garden marker can be made using a house flooring beam or joist. The beam is set with six teeth made from pointed fence stakes or common pickets. This adaptive re-use of available materials produced a laborsaving tool at no cost.

Following Watson's description, the curator of collections at Old World Wisconsin and a skilled volunteer worked together to make a garden marker for use in the sizable 1860 James and Rebecca Sanford Farm kitchen garden. Assembled from a joist similar to those found under the Sanford house's flooring and set with pickets from fencing that surrounds the exhibit, the garden marker incorporates themes related to planting techniques, building construction methods, and fencing styles in one object.

Yankee writers recommended that vegetables be planted in straight rows and kept cleanly hoed. A board fence surrounds the garden.
GERALD H. EMMERICH JR.

them. The perennial asparagus and rhubarb (or pieplant) maintained a permanent location. Lettuce, cress, endive, kale, spinach, and sorrel sometimes joined the garden layout; interestingly, these salad greens rarely came to the Yankee table uncooked. Potatoes, pumpkins, corn, and vegetables for animal feed usually grew with field crops, beyond the kitchen garden's borders.

Early Yankee kitchen gardens often included many familiar herbs. The most commonly grown for culinary use included anise, lemon balm, basil, caraway, coriander, dill, fennel, sweet marjoram, parsley, rosemary, sage, summer and winter savory, spearmint, thyme, and lemon thyme. Herbs grown for their medicinal value included chamomile, elecampane, horehound, hyssop, American pennyroyal, and wormwood. Lavender enjoyed great popularity, much appreciated for its fragrance. The herbs were gathered when in bloom, tied in small bunches, hung in the shade to dry thoroughly, and then stored in airtight boxes or jars. Nasturtiums grew cheerfully among the vegetables: their flowers and peppery leaves were added to salads, and their young flower buds and "berries"—seeds gathered while still young and green—pickled in vinegar made a good substitute for capers.[3] Calendulas (or pot marigolds) found a multitude of uses. Often grown as ornamentals to brighten the garden, their flower petals added color to soups and stews and relieved skin irritations when added to salves and steeped in water for bathing.

Clockwise, from top left:
Large Red tomatoes or "love apples"
GERALD H. EMMERICH JR.

Red Fig tomatoes historically were dried and used as dried fruit or pickled.
GERALD H. EMMERICH JR.

Yellow Crookneck squash, a pleasant summer squash, was popular with the Yankees.
NANCY L. KLEMP

Green Nutmeg melon, one of the most popular muskmelons in the 1860s, has sweet-flavored pale green flesh.
SANDRA MATSON

The Citron melon or Citron watermelon is an early ancestor of the watermelon. The very firm white flesh can be cut into pieces and cooked in sugar syrup to make the American version of candied citron, which is used as a dried fruit.
GERALD H. EMMERICH JR.

Queen Anne's Pocket Melon matures to a size that fits comfortably in a lady's hand or pocket. Grown for its fragrance of sweet melons, one or two placed in a bowl or basket will fill a room with a sweet aroma. This melon was more beloved for its fragrance than its flavor.
NANCY L. KLEMP

GARDEN HOES

Gardeners protected their investment in seeds and hope for a bountiful harvest by vigilantly weeding and cultivating their growing plants. Hoeing not only destroyed weeds but also loosened the soil, enabling it to retain moisture. It was an essential chore and prompted the manufacture of hoes in different patterns and sizes to meet special cultivating needs and soil conditions. For example, the single straight-bladed thrust hoe was designed for shallow hoeing in light soil to dislodge small weeds. The crane's bill hoe, shaped like a tapered stake, was styled to loosen soil at a deeper depth.

Two hoes in particular were mainstays in the nineteenth-century kitchen garden. The first was the centuries-old planters' hoe, identified by its wide, flat blade designed for both hoeing deep in loose earth and breaking through crusty soils. Primarily used when rough and vigorous cultivation was needed, the planters' hoe is not discussed at any length in nineteenth-century garden manuals. Perhaps the authors thought it too obvious a style, preferring instead to highlight hoes with specific functions. Their reading audience of prosperous rural farmers and urban kitchen gardeners could afford to purchase a recommended selection of cultivating implements. At Old World Wisconsin, planters' hoes are heavily used in the gardens of first-settler

CAST STEEL PLANTERS' HOES.

Half Polished, Round Eye.

No. 00, width of Blade $6\frac{1}{2}$ in., size of Eye $1\frac{3}{4}\times1\frac{1}{2}$ in....per dozen, $
No. 0, width of Blade 7 in., size of Eye $1\frac{7}{8}\times1\frac{5}{8}$ in.... "
No. 1, width of Blade $7\frac{1}{2}$ in., size of Eye $1\frac{7}{8}\times1\frac{5}{8}$ in.... "
No. 2, width of Blade 8 in., size of Eye $2\times1\frac{3}{4}$ in.... "
No. 3, width of Blade $8\frac{1}{2}$ in., size of Eye $2\times1\frac{3}{4}$ in.... "
No. 4, width of Blade 9 in., size of Eye $2\frac{1}{8}\times1\frac{7}{8}$ in.... "
No. 5, width of Blade $9\frac{1}{2}$ in., size of Eye $2\frac{1}{8}\times1\frac{7}{8}$ in.... "

Full Polished, Round Eye.

No. 00, width of Blade $6\frac{1}{2}$ in., size of Eye $1\frac{3}{4}\times1\frac{1}{2}$ in..per dozen, $
No. 0, width of Blade 7 in., size of Eye $1\frac{7}{8}\times1\frac{5}{8}$ in.. "
No. 1, width of Blade $7\frac{1}{2}$ in., size of Eye $1\frac{7}{8}\times1\frac{5}{8}$ in.. "
No. 2, width of Blade 8 in., size of Eye $2\times1\frac{3}{4}$ in.. "
No. 3, width of Blade $8\frac{1}{2}$ in., size of Eye $2\times1\frac{3}{4}$ in.. "
No. 4, width of Blade 9 in., size of Eye $2\frac{1}{8}\times1\frac{7}{8}$ in.. "
No. 5, width of Blade $9\frac{1}{2}$ in., size of Eye $2\frac{1}{8}\times1\frac{7}{8}$ in.. "

Illustration of a planters' hoe offered for sale, 1865

ILLUSTRATED CATALOGUE OF AMERICAN HARDWARE OF THE RUSSELL AND ERWIN MANUFACTURING CO.

GARDEN HOES

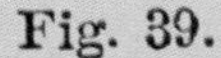

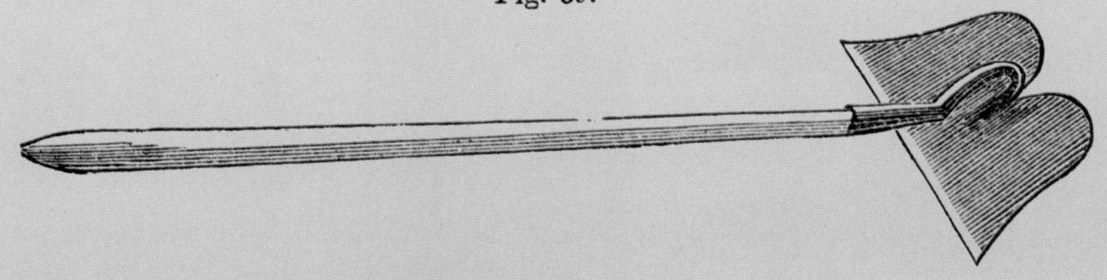

Goose-necked steel Garden-hoe.

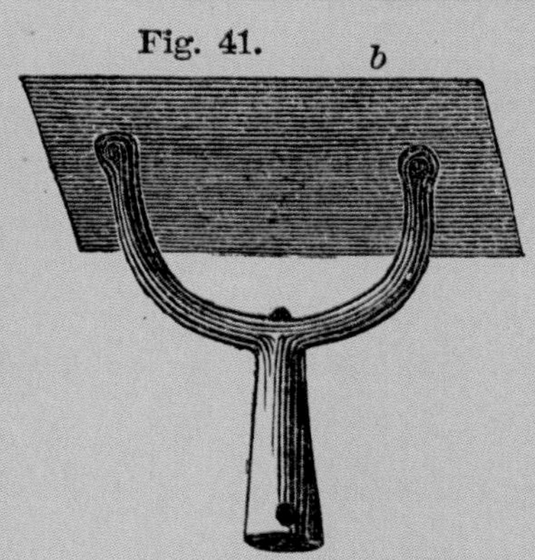

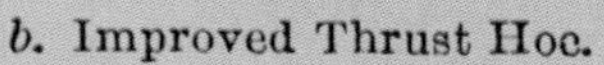

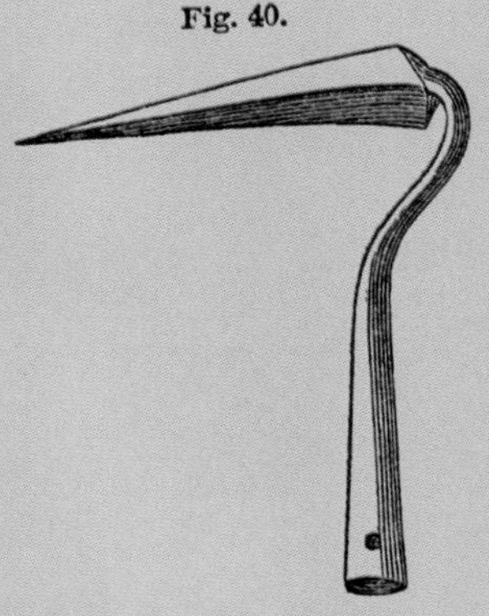

Goose-necked crane's-bill Hoe, or Weeding-hoe.

Goose-necked, thrust, and crane's bill hoes, 1859
ALEXANDER WATSON, *THE AMERICAN HOME GARDEN*

families, for whom limited cash flow restricted the purchase of manufactured goods to universal basics such as the planters' hoe.

The goose-necked garden hoe introduced by the mid-nineteenth century represents a refinement in hoe design. Its bell-shaped blade is welded to a gooseneck-shaped shank or stem. The upper blade is distinctively wing-shaped—this was an improvement in design that balanced the blade, giving the gardener greater control of the hoe. Whether drawing soil at the corner or center of the blade, the hoe did not wobble. It became the common hoe of the nineteenth century.

Among the garden tools at the 1860 James and Rebecca Sanford Farm is the innovative-for-its-time goose-necked hoe. It hangs nearby what was then the still-useful but old-style planters' hoe.

The flowers, leaves, and young seeds of the nasturtium plant are all useful in the kitchen.
GERALD H. EMMERICH JR.

Opposite page: Calendulas, or pot marigolds, have culinary, medicinal, and ornamental value.
TERRY MOLTER

Flowers were sometimes included in the kitchen garden enclosure, often in separate beds for cutting. Among the many choices, asters, balsam, candytuft, carnations, delphinium, larkspur, mignonette, snapdragons, stock, and zinnias grew as seasonal cut flowers to fill vases and brighten the house. Ferns and scented geranium leaves provided a soft backdrop for the lovely floral arrangements. Everlasting flowers such as ammobium, amaranthus, acroclinium, celosia, gomphrena, helichrysum, and nigella retained their form and color for years when grown, collected, and hung to dry in a dark, airy location. These became welcome winter bouquets. Decorative grasses added a delicate touch to the floral pieces.

Enthusiastic gardeners sometimes edged the kitchen garden paths with curled parsley, portulaca, alyssum, or other low-growing flowers to create an attractive and inviting display.

The overall size of the Yankee kitchen garden varied widely, partially dependent on the number of people it was intended to support. Inns and establishments responsible for feeding a steady clientele sometimes maintained gardens of several acres. By contrast, a family kitchen garden planted on one-quarter acre or even less was not uncommon. Garden work was generally done by hand, although in the larger farm gardens the plow often assisted with soil cultivation. Management of the kitchen garden generally fell

Fragrant rose-scented geraniums have been popular for centuries. Deep red perilla was introduced in the early 1860s as an attractive plant for bedding and bouquets.
NANCY L. KLEMP

A bed of everlasting flowers for winter bouquets
NANCY L. KLEMP

Potted plants grace the formal parlor at the James and Rebecca Sanford House. An intricate arrangement of wax flowers and leaves, protected by a glass dome, is visible on the right.
MIKE MORBECK

among the farmwife's responsibilities, which included the preparation and storage of food as well as the washing and sewing of most of the family's clothing. Apparently most Yankee women feared there was something rustic, unfeminine, and unrefined about outdoor work, and they preferred spending their time indoors, pursuing more genteel and artistic endeavors. Those who hired domestic servants—a not uncommon practice in Yankee households[4]—could oversee the gardening activity without worrying about too much physical involvement, rough hands, or a complexion discolored by the sun. While many upstanding Yankee women shied away from laboring in the garden, they had no objection to cutting and arranging floral bouquets. Many also developed a passion for indoor gardening, where they used potted plants to beautify the home.

Through the 1860s, decorative flower or shrub beds, when grown, were laid out in the familiar geometric patterns and situated within the confines of the fenced dooryard. Yankee housewives wanted gardens reminiscent of those they had left behind in the Northeast.

Entire volumes were written about the much-loved roses, long considered the queen of all flowers. A popular and informative 1880 garden publication noted: "The Rose, the

THE GARDEN ENGINE

The modern-day garden hose is a miraculous piece of equipment often taken for granted. Consider not having such a tool and needing to deliver water to the garden when rainfall isn't sufficient to keep plants alive. This was the plight of nineteenth-century gardeners. They used watering-pots and buckets carried by hand from the well, river, or stream. This method of transporting water was laborious, especially for large garden plots, nurseries, and greenhouses. As early as the 1850s, however, an ingenious machine called a "garden engine" was introduced to lessen the burden.

The basic garden engine design was a thirty- to fifty-gallon watertight metal box with wheelbarrow-style handles, two wide-rimmed front wheels, two rear legs, and a simple pumping mechanism. The engine was wheeled down the garden path much like a wheelbarrow. Simpler designs were made of wood instead of metal. Fancier models incorporated decorative cast-iron parts and extra features such as a siphoning hose that made it easier to refill the water-box with water from a nearby pond or stream. With a capacity to throw water to a height of well over fifty feet, garden engines often doubled as small fire engines. This feature was not lost on the author of *The New Hampshire Kitchen, Fruit, and Floral Gardener* (1852): "They [garden engines] are used extensively in gardens, nurseries, &c., and are sometimes found to afford very valuable assistance in case of fire."[1]

Few rural Wisconsin families of the nineteenth century had the means to purchase a garden engine. Materials found on the farm such as a used molasses or kerosene barrel fitted with handles and mounted between two old wheels could be fabricated as a water carrier. However, at Old World Wisconsin's re-creation of the 1860 James and Rebecca Sanford farmstead with its substantial kitchen garden, a simple model garden engine made by a skilled volunteer in collaboration with the curator of collections and historical gardener reflects the

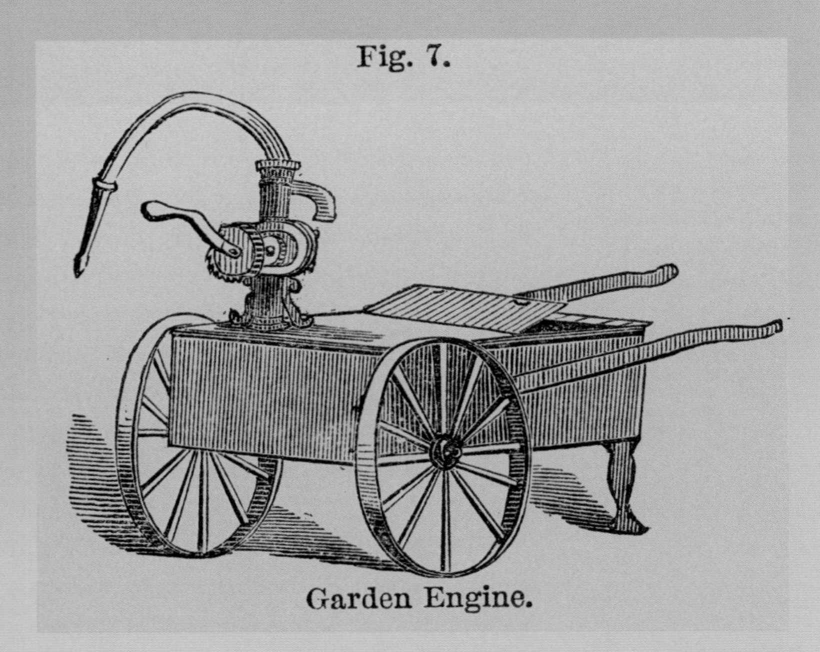

Garden engine illustration from *The American Home Garden*, 1859

THE GARDEN ENGINE

Reproduction garden engine at Old World Wisconsin SANDRA MATSON

family's prosperity. Its design was primarily extrapolated from an illustration in the 1859 publication *The American Home Garden*, although many other period illustrations were also consulted. Museum visitors accustomed to turning on a faucet and pointing a hose are invited to hand-crank the garden engine pump. This action sends water through the pump's black India rubber hosing and onto the garden beds. Nothing deepens our appreciation of modern convenience as much as experiencing an exhausting alternative.

NOTE

1. E. M. Tubbs, *The New Hampshire Kitchen, Fruit, and Floral Gardener* (Peterboro, NH: K. C. Scott, 1852), 14.

The rose, queen of flowers: the pale yellow rose, top left, is Cornelia Cook, a tea rose. Three Bourbon roses complete the bouquet; the deep red is Queen of Bedders, the pink is Hermosa, and the pale lower rose is Souvenir de la Malmaison. According to the June 1882 issue of *Vick's Illustrated Monthly Magazine*, these were all "monthly" roses popular that year.

universal favorite flower of all nations and ages, never loses it popularity, and always commands, as it deserves, a prominent place and devoted attention in all good gardens."[5] Writers of the day often recommended these treasures be grown in beds made up solely of roses, sometimes segregated by color and laid out in a pattern of beds forming the shape of a rosary.

Evergreens and individual shrubs often were planted as specimens within the dooryard, each standing alone so that it might be shown to best advantage.

Interest in fruit growing was keen from the early years of settlement. Pioneers planted apple trees and quickly learned that the familiar eastern varieties were no match for the harsh Upper Midwestern climate. They undertook extensive experimentation and breeding and established nurseries. At least ten nurseries were in operation in southeastern Wisconsin as early as 1851.[6]

Writers frequently promoted the implementation of the responsible agricultural practices of liberally manuring fields and rotating crops on farmland, but Yankees did not necessarily follow through with the recommendations. Profit was often more a motivating factor than was some deeply felt love of or tie to the land.

Andrew Jackson Downing (1815–1852), considered by many to be the first great American landscape gardener, authored *Treatise on the Theory and Practice of Landscape Gardening, Cottage Residences, Fruits and Fruit Trees of America* and founded the periodical *The Horticulturist.* As early as 1851, he warned: "It does not require much scrutiny on the part of a serious inquirer, to discover that we are in some respects like a large and increasing family, running over and devouring a great estate to which they have fallen heirs, with little or no care to preserve or maintain it, rather than a wise and prudent one, seeking to maintain that estate in its best and most productive condition." There is, he continued, a "miserable system of farming steadily pursued by eight-tenths of all farmers in this country, since its first settlement; a system which proceeds upon the principle of taking as many crops from the land with as little manure as possible—until its productive powers are exhausted, and then—emigrating to some part of the country where they can apply the same practice to a new soil . . . the emigration is always 'to THE WEST.' " Downing went on to write, "There are, doubtless, many superficial thinkers, who consider these western soils exhaustless. . . . There was never a greater fallacy."[7]

Unfortunately, Yankee farmers too often gave even less attention to their kitchen gardens than they did to their field crops. Numerous periodicals and books commented on the sorry situation. "We are surprised when we consider how few good gardens there are among farmers," observed an 1854 Wisconsin farm periodical.[8] Five years later Henry Ward Beecher wrote, "Farmers are apt to have very inferior gardens."[9] The concern continued, as noted in an article published in 1896: "On the farm there is nothing more neglected than the vegetable garden. A farmer will grow mangels for his cows and carrots for his horses, so as to give them a change of food during the long winter, thus keeping them in good health. But the importance of having an abundance and variety of vegetables for his family, is by many entirely overlooked."[10]

Writers increasingly recommended that their readers plant their kitchen crops in rows so the produce might be mechanically cultivated, thus saving time and labor. This planting style became a symbol of Americanization in a country where land was plentiful. It represented a marked contrast to the old-fashioned space-saving but labor-intensive European practice of gardening in beds.

James Harvey Sanford, of Camden, New York, an eighth-generation American, and his wife, Rebecca, from Dover, Ohio, traveled to Wisconsin as newlyweds in 1841. They purchased land and built a log cabin in the Town of Richmond, Walworth County. In 1845 the Sanfords bought 153 acres in the nearby Town of LaGrange and built a large, handsome house in the Greek Revival style so popular in the East. By 1860 they owned 190 acres, farmed mainly cash grain crops supplemented with additional crops in lesser amounts, and maintained livestock, including sheep for wool. A successful farmer, Sanford also held positions in local politics and was active in the church community and the construction of a local schoolhouse.

In addition to James and Rebecca, the household in 1860 included five children, two farm laborers, and two domestic servant girls. A woman of Mrs. Sanford's stature (she had attended Oberlin College in northeastern Ohio years earlier), who lived in a fine home with a civic-minded family active in the community, likely entertained frequently and had much to oversee.

The James and Rebecca Sanford home, Town of LaGrange, Walworth County, circa 1875
WHI IMAGE ID 74638

The James and Rebecca Sanford House, moved to Old World Wisconsin and restored to its 1860 appearance
TERRY MOLTER

Relocated to Old World Wisconsin in 1981, the Sanford home has been restored to its 1860 appearance. The landscape, including the Yankee kitchen garden, has been carefully researched and re-created to illustrate the home grounds of a farm family of the Sanfords' affluence and social standing.

Enclosed by a horizontal board fence, the home's large garden, situated adjacent to the house and convenient to the kitchen, contains the vegetables and herbs deemed necessary to support a Yankee farmer's household. In addition, the flower beds would have provided Mrs. Sanford with fresh bouquets for summer and dried ones for winter, to adorn her home's interior.

2
A Taste for Embellishment

In the years following the Civil War the yields and profitability of wheat farming declined sharply due to decreasing soil fertility as well as disease and insect infestation in the crop that had been the mainstay for Wisconsin farmers since the 1840s. Adding insult to injury, wheat flourished farther west, and the newly expanded railroad provided easy transportation of that crop. The price dropped. With wheat farming no longer a profitable enterprise, Yankee farmers sought alternatives. Some moved west to continue cashing in on "king wheat." Some diversified their operations in search of different successful cash crops; their efforts were redirected to numerous alternatives including rye, oats, hops, and tobacco. Others turned their focus to animal husbandry. Sheep were raised for wool, and by the late 1870s many found success in dairy farming.

Many families totally relinquished life on the farm, looking instead to villages and cities. The Yankees who joined this urban movement continued their active interest in schools, churches, and government and sought new opportunities with great Yankee entrepreneurial spirit. They found employment in their new communities, and some opened their own businesses. The prospect of becoming businesspeople and specialists appealed to them. In the 1870s, Yankees in Fort Atkinson, for example, proudly ran the bank, the newspaper, the major centers of lodging and entertainment, and many other commercial and industrial operations.[1]

Living in town on smaller plots of land, these Yankees found it necessary to rethink their yards and gardens. With produce now available for purchase from local markets, families no longer needed to raise all their own food, and as manufactured products became available and affordable, growing medicinal herbs and dye plants in the home garden quickly fell out of fashion.

Previous spread:
The brilliant gold blossoms of a perennial helianthus add embellishment to the landscape of the Wesley and Sophia Benson home grounds re-created at Old World Wisconsin. In addition to adding a decorative appearance, they serve to screen the view of the utilitarian kitchen garden from passersby.
MIKE MORBECK

Fragrant white alyssum edges the front of this re-created Yankee village kitchen garden. Deep red perilla keeps company with a small assortment of favorite flowers grown to be cut for bouquets. In addition to providing produce for the table, tomato plants supported by wooden stakes and pole beans add vertical interest.
GERALD H. EMMERICH JR.

The kitchen garden grew smaller and was relegated to the backyard, a private family space behind the house, sometimes screened from public view by a board fence or shrub plantings. Any work-related activities, including vegetable gardening, took place in this area. Laid out in a square or rectangular shape, the kitchen garden featured a central path for easy accessibility, and vegetables grew in beds familiar to generations of Yankees. Beans thrived in bush form or climbed up decorative towers; beets, carrots, parsnips, turnips, cabbage, lettuce, peas, spinach, onions, and tomatoes all occupied their own beds. Potatoes, pumpkins, and sweet corn, which required considerable growing space, tended to be purchased rather than grown in the family garden.

Fruit continued to be popular, and folks often made room for pieplant (rhubarb), a couple of apple trees, and numerous small fruits, such as currants, raspberries, and strawberries. Turned into jams, jellies, preserves, pies, and puddings, fruits were welcome at the table, at social gatherings, and as entries in local fairs.

The front yard became the face shown to the public—in effect, the garden parlor. This area, in theory, was grown for pleasure; in actuality it often became a means of winning the admiration of neighbors and passersby.

Lawns of grass finely sheared and rolled to look like green velvet became desirable but presented a maintenance challenge. Before the 1870s, the scythe was the grass-cutting tool of choice, with grass hook or sickle touch-ups for tight spots and along

This drawing from the 1873 Walworth County atlas shows the Francis Dillon house fashionably landscaped. Decorative flower beds were cut into a lawn of grass, specimen trees and shrubs dotted the yard, and vining plants framed the porch. WHI IMAGE ID 77049

THE LAWN MOWERS

Centuries-old fascinations with the aesthetics of gardening and a bit of borrowed technology from the textile trade led to the invention of the lawn mower by an English textile mill engineer in 1830. Lawn maintenance was traditionally very labor intensive. Men used hand scythes and grass sickles or managed grazing animals to keep lawns cut low and even. In early-nineteenth-century America, a sweeping lawn was a prominent symbol of wealth and status. The lawn mower eventually changed this perception by democratizing the notion that only the well-to-do could find pleasure in their front yard.

Lawn mowers were well advertised in America as early as the 1870s, but their general acceptance was slow, due primarily to their high cost. An illustration of the "Archimedean Revolving Cutter" mower in the March 1875 issue of the *American Agriculturist, for the Farm, Garden & Household* pictures a young woman using the machine on the manicured grounds of a well-established middle-class residence; this was not your average American dwelling. The same model mower sold for $18 in an 1872 seed catalog.[1] In comparison, a simple grass hook or sickle sold in the same 1872 catalog for just 75 cents.[2] It would take until late in the nineteenth century for the price of lawn mowers to fall within reach of small-town Americans. As mowers became affordable to more people, the aesthetics of lawn care rooted deeply in American culture.

The "Archimedean Revolving Cutter" lawn mower was named in reference to the Greek mathematician Archimedes because it incorporated a revolving screw-shaped blade inside a cylinder—the essential design of the Archimedean screw. This 1875 advertisement for the machine emphasized—in italic and capitalized type—that "by the action of the revolving cutter the grass is *cut into small particles and evenly scattered* on the ground where it is cut, NEVER LOOKING UNSIGHTLY." Thus began America's preoccupation with meticulous lawn care.

AMERICAN AGRICULTURIST, FOR THE FARM, GARDEN & HOUSEHOLD, VOL. 34, NO. 3 (NEW YORK: ORANGE JUDD COMPANY, MARCH 1875)

NOTES

1. *B. K. Bliss and Son's Illustrated Spring Catalogue and Amateurs Guide to the Flower and Kitchen Garden* (New York: B. K. Bliss & Son, 1872), 107.

2. Ibid., 111–113.

This collection of annual flowers appeared in an 1876 garden publication: 1. Striped petunia; 2. Pansy; 3. Japan cockscomb; 4. Nemophila; 5. Camellia balsam; 6. Double portulaca; 7. Varieties of *Phlox drummondii*; 8. Ten-weeks stock

VICK'S FLOWER AND VEGETABLE GARDEN

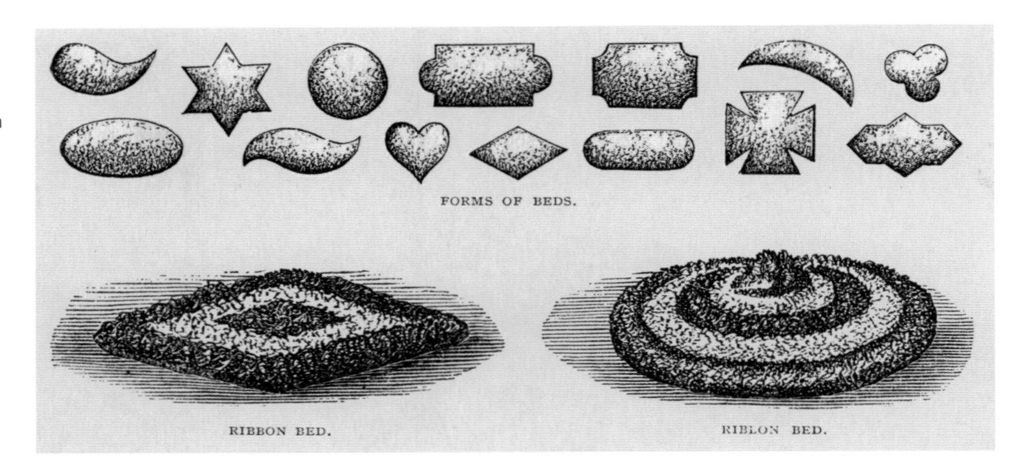

Decorative flower beds filled with colorful annuals planted to look like stripes in ribbon enhanced the front lawns of fashion-conscious nineteenth-century Midwestern Yankees.

VICK'S FLOWER AND VEGETABLE GARDEN, [1880?]

When arranged into bouquets, carefully dried garden blossoms and wild grasses enhanced a home's interior year-round.

THE LADIES' FLORAL CABINET AND PICTORIAL HOME COMPANION 5, JUNE 1876

fences. With the invention of the lawn mower in England in 1830 and its introduction to America in 1855, the dream of a lovely lawn became possible. By the early 1870s catalogs advertised lawn mowers for sale, although due to their pricing at $16 (making an eleven-inch cut) to $30 (for a whopping eighteen-inch cut)[2] they were not affordable to everyone. (The price for scythes started at $1.50; grass hooks were 75 cents.)[3]

The Andrew Proudfit House in Madison, circa 1875: carefully landscaped beds cut into a manicured grass lawn, decorative vines, and hanging baskets on the porch indicate popular design trends.
WHI IMAGE ID 27033

In addition, the early newfangled lawn mowers worked well only on level ground, further limiting their practicality.

Beds of colorful annual flowers were popular in the Upper Midwest through the end of the nineteenth century. A circle, diamond, star, or some other fanciful shape could be artistically cut into the front lawn and filled with plants arranged to display masses of nonstop color throughout the season. A bed might consist of plants all of one kind, segregated by color, or of a few different kinds set out in groups to give the appearance of stripes in ribbons, a style known as "ribbon bedding." These gardens frequently featured geraniums, pansies, petunias, annual Drummond's phlox, portulaca, and verbenas as their star performers, and they were for adornment only: no cut flowers from the carpet beds, please!

Garden authorities recommended "just back of the lawn"[4] as the place for generous beds of flowers for cutting. Stems of alyssum, balsam, candytuft, larkspur, mignonette, perilla, pinks, stock, zinnias, and many others could be gathered for fresh bouquets. Acroclinium, ammobium, gomphrena, gypsophila, helichrysum, helipterum, statice, and xeranthemum frequently were grown to be cut and dried for use in winter bouquets.

Beds of perennial flowers and bulb gardens were recognized as interesting and worth growing but not proper candidates for the front yard. These tend to bloom only once in a season, and for a limited time, "and therefore are not suited for the lawn, where a continuous show of flowers is absolutely necessary; but in a position a little retired, like the border of the lawn, or in its rear, nothing can be more interesting, more beautiful, or more instructive."[5] Perennials gained popularity at the turn of the century, as did the use of native plants in the landscape: indigenous bergamot, blazing star, butterfly weed, coneflowers, phlox, and violets were among those considered to be worthy additions to the flower garden. Roses continued to be nostalgic favorites, and new varieties being introduced received a warm welcome. Horticultural periodical articles rated newly

The morning glory, a favorite flowering vine grown by early Wisconsin immigrants to beautify the home
GERALD H. EMMERICH JR.

introduced roses for their beauty, form, color, and fragrance. Repeat bloomers were especially valued.

As homeowners gained enthusiasm for outdoor gardening, purposefully planted vining plants were encouraged to climb over porches and around doors and windows. In 1875, Mrs. S. O. Johnson, author of *Every Woman Her Own Flower Gardener*, ardently suggested, "We must have vines, an abundance of vines. A house without vines is like a bird without a mate; it wears a look of desolation."[6] The scarlet runner bean, morning glory, clematis, grapevine, Dutchman's-pipe, ivy, and Virginia creeper, among others, skyrocketed into popularity as vining plants came into vogue.

Women received great encouragement to venture outside and participate in the gardening activity. Authors of books and magazine articles and even editors of seed catalogs appealed to the Yankee woman's high sense of morality, connection to family, and concern with good health and quality-of-life issues, hoping to instill pleasure and pride—and participation—in flower gardening out-of-doors. An 1876 seed catalog advocated: "Ladies should cultivate flowers as an invigorating and inspiring out-door occupation. Many are pining and dying from monotony and depression, who might bury their cares by planting a few seeds, and secure bloom in their cheeks by their culture. In the family, flowers are quite indispensible to domestic sunshine."[7] In *Every Woman Her Own Flower Gardener*, Mrs. Johnson noted, "A beautiful garden, tastefully laid out and well kept, is a certain evidence of taste, refinement, and culture. It makes a lowly cottage attractive, and lends a charm to the stateliest palace."[8] She goes on to say, "American women live in-doors too much, and thus sacrifice their health and spirits. They cultivate neuralgia, dyspepsia, and all their attendant ills—rather than the beautiful and glorious flowers which God has scattered so abundantly all over the world."[9]

A bouquet of perennial flowers popular in 1876: 1. Everlasting pea; 2. Carnations; 3. *Adonis autumnalis*; 4. Pentstemon [*sic*]; 5. Sweet William; 6–7. Larkspur; 8–9. Digitalis; 10. Aquilegia

VICK'S FLOWER AND VEGETABLE GARDEN

YANKEE LADIES TO THE GARDEN

Labor in her own garden? How was a proper Yankee lady even to contemplate such a radical idea? While numerous volumes described beautiful gardens to be admired and enjoyed, the concept of a proper lady doing the physical work herself was new. The 1875 edition of the first gardening book written *by* an American woman directed *to* women offered great encouragement and detailed information on how to go about it. Under the nom de plume "Daisy Eyebright," Mrs. S. O. Johnson wrote *Every Woman Her Own Flower Gardener*. She understood the need for assistance with heavy work and the necessity of becoming acclimated to outdoor work, and she included advice on appropriate attire and tools for the venture.

In the first chapter, Mrs. Johnson assures her readers:

> *To be sure, Pat O'Shovelem's aid is needful to prepare the ground, lay out the beds, and harden the walks; but, gentler, smaller hands can plant the seeds and roots, can keep down the weeds, tie up, stake, train, water and prune.*

The garden fork is useful for loosening ground, removing plants, and uprooting weeds.
NANCY L. KLEMP

> *I have little faith in American women becoming farmers,—holding the plow—wielding the spade or the shovel; but I do know from long experience, that all the rest of the work can be accomplished by women, if they possess a love for the beautiful.*
>
> *Women can find strength to cultivate a garden successfully, if they will commence by degrees. . . . Garden by degrees, my friends, and cultivate your muscles, with your plants! An hour, or even half an hour, is long enough for a commencement, and the next day extend the time ten minutes, and so on, until you can work for three, or even six hours in succession.*
>
> *But take it easy; provide an old piece of carpeting to kneel upon while planting, or weeding with a fork; and if your knees are not accustomed to that position, humor them by placing an empty raisin or soap box upon the carpet, and sit upon that;—and if a cushion would also be agreeable, cover a small pillow with some dark chintz, and place that on the box.*

YANKEE LADIES TO THE GARDEN

Now you will have a luxurious seat, and can garden without a sense of pain; yet don't stay too long, nor become too much heated. *The carpeting protects the skirts from the dampness of the soil, and should always be used. It can be kept conveniently at hand, with the box and the cushion.*

Of course, flounces, puffs, and furbelows, with their accompanying upper skirts, are not suitable for such occupations. A dark chintz dress is the best, for it can go into the wash-tub when it is in need of cleansing. A woolen bathing dress makes an excellent garden costume—for skirts are always in the way. If it is admissible on the beach where wealth and fashion do congregate, why not in the garden, surrounding one's house?

A large shade hat, and a pair of old kid gloves are indispensable. Rubber gloves are often recommended, but are far too clumsy for the fingers.

Now, the dress is bespoken, and we must purchase the tools required. A large three-pronged iron fork, with a short handle, is needful for loosening the ground, removing plants and uprooting weeds. I should rather do without a trowel than such a fork. They can be purchased of all hardware dealers.

A small set of tools, comprising a rake and hoe on one handle, a trowel, and a spade, are very essential. With their aid much light work can be accomplished without calling upon Mr. O'Shovelem.

A watering pot, with a large nozzle, and a fine sprinkler, is also required.

With these imple-ments, every woman can be her own gardener— *and not only raise all the flowers she may desire, but also contribute a large share of the vegetables that are always welcomed at the table, during both summer and winter.*[1]

The trowel played an important part in the nineteenth-century gardener's tool kit.
NANCY L. KLEMP

With these preliminaries taken care of, Mrs. Johnson went on to share numerous chapters of sound horticultural advice.

NOTE

1. Mrs. S. O. Johnson, *Every Woman Her Own Flower Gardener* (New York: Henry T. Williams, 1875), 6–8.

GARDEN SETS

Specialized sets of garden tools designed exclusively for use by women and children made their appearance in the post–Civil War era as gardening for pleasure gained in popularity. "Floral Sets," "Children's Garden Sets," and "Ladies' Garden Sets" typically combined a hoe, a spade, and a rake, each scaled down in size to half the length of standard garden implements.

"They are very useful to a lady or to the juvenile cultivator," read an endorsement of the "Ladies' and Children's Garden Set" in the 1871 *Garden and Field Seeds & Grains Catalog.*[1] This set sold for $1.75, more than four times the cost of a single standard-size hoe priced at 40 cents in the same catalog. Garden sets were expensive, nonessential tools more apt to be owned by a lady of leisure in a village setting than a rural farm family. Mrs. Sophia Benson and her young grandson Charlie might have enjoyed using a set of these downsized tools. Young visitors to Old World Wisconsin are encouraged to do the same in the garden of the restored Wesley and Sophia Benson home. For many, the hands-on activity of hoeing, raking, or spading marks their first experience in a garden.

NOTE

1. *R. H. Allen & Co.'s Garden and Field Seeds & Grains Catalog* (New York: R. H. Allen & Company, 1871), 44.

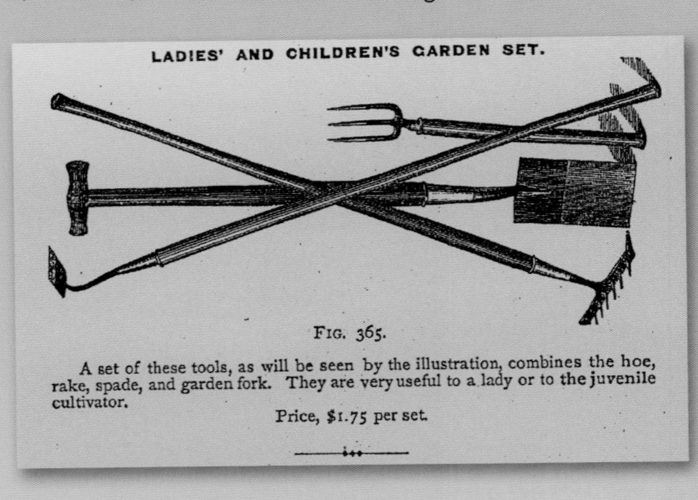
LADIES' AND CHILDREN'S GARDEN SET.

FIG. 365.

A set of these tools, as will be seen by the illustration, combines the hoe, rake, spade, and garden fork. They are very useful to a lady or to the juvenile cultivator.

Price, $1.75 per set.

Garden sets consisted of a hoe, rake, and spade scaled down in size for use by children and ladies. This set advertised for sale in 1871 also included a garden fork.

R. H. ALLEN & CO. 1871 RETAIL PRICED CATALOGUE OF GARDEN AND FIELD SEEDS & GRAINS

A reproduction ladies' and children's garden set at Old World Wisconsin

TERRY MOLTER

The home of Wesley and Sophia Benson, moved from Fort Atkinson to Old World Wisconsin and restored to its 1875 appearance
TERRY MOLTER

Wesley P. Benson, his wife, Sophia, and two children traveled from Vermont to Koshkonong in Jefferson County in 1845. By the late 1850s they had two additional children, farmed at a modest level, and bred livestock, with a special interest in horses, for more than fifteen years. The family left the farm in 1861, and Benson began work as a blacksmith in the village of Fort Atkinson, a prosperous, well-established community. They purchased land and within a year built a balloon-frame house, a style typical of a working man in a village.[10] Their tastefully decorated Yankee home included a separate parlor and ladies' sitting room—a space devoted to entertaining, where a lady of culture, taste, and training might pursue the decorative arts. She could undertake fine needlework, paper embroidery, calligraphy, painting, the creation of blossoms from wax or feathers, or the construction of bouquets of fresh or dried flowers and grasses.

By 1875 Benson had retired from blacksmithing but apparently continued a long-held interest in breeding and racing trotting horses. The couple's widowed twenty-eight-year-old daughter, Emma Barney, and her six-year-old son, Charlie, moved in with her

WINDOW GARDENING

Although most Yankee women needed encouragement to garden outdoors, they had no such qualms about indoor window gardening. Viewed as a perfectly acceptable activity for a lady or gentleman, horticulture and the care of houseplants brought respect and admiration from acquaintances who recognized the talent required—as with all things of beauty and refinement—to tastefully decorate the home with plants. Whether the individual was well-to-do or just scraping by, the sense of accomplishment and joy felt by the caretaker of happy potted plants should not be undervalued. When the weather outside was unpleasant, or when the indoor plants were blooming, the pleasure was multiplied.

To gain a better appreciation for the challenges the nineteenth-century indoor gardener faced, consider caring for potted plants without central heating. In *The Ladies' Floral Cabinet and Pictorial Home Companion*, a monthly magazine for ladies that proclaimed itself to be "the handsomest illustrated journal of household art, flowers and home literature in America,"[1] a reader shared her winter indoor gardening experience:

> *I must give some directions how to hasten plants into bloom, to the many who have no regular artificial heat for them.*
> *We sometimes have many cold and cloudy days in succession, when our plants seem to refuse to open or produce buds; then take a medium sized vessel containing boiling water (the little "boiler" with open top, in which "John" heats his shaving-water now, and cooked eggs and oysters in his unhallowed bachelor days, will do) and put a flower-pot saucer on top of it, and set your plant in that; let it remain until the water gets cold (it will remain hot a long time if you keep it in the same vessel in which it was heated), and repeat the process two or three times a day, and you will "see a difference." Don't be afraid of the hot water. The heat is just right by the time it penetrates both saucer and pot. This is also an excellent way to hasten the formation of roots to cuttings, especially in cool weather.*
>
> *The next best "forcing" process is to place an inch deep layer of powdered charcoal on the surface of the pots; black absorbs heat, and you will find when the sun's rays fall on your plants that the earth in the charcoaled pots is much warmer than in the others.*
> *Keep your plants away from fire-heat. Have them as far from stove and grate as possible, and never think of bringing them near the fire to "keep them from freezing." If the thermometer "starts" towards zero, put them under a table in the middle of the room, and pin blankets closely around and over them—put them in your wardrobe—anywhere to keep the frost from them. Raise the window, or carry them out-doors, on the south side of your house, every mild day,* i.e., *whenever the thermometer stands*

(continued on page 38)

WINDOW GARDENING

A LITTLE SUMMER ALL SHUT IN.

I.

'Tis sweet to have, when the storms begin
To roam o'er the earth so wide,
A little summer, all shut in
From the frozen world outside;
A little summer, all our own,
From the days when the robins go,
To the days when they come from a warmer zone,
And the Pansies peep from the snow.

II.

The rich may daily on dainties dine,
And daily on velvet tread,
But give to my home the trailing vine,
And the blooming flowers instead;
A cheerful wife, in a sunny room,
Who sings as she flits about;
What care I, then, with the plants in bloom,
For the wintry winds without.

III.

How sweet to come from the constant din
Of life's contending tide,
To my little summer, all shut in,
From the frozen world outside;
To watch the bright Geraniums grow,
From the bud to the opening flower,
While the outer world lies under the snow,
And bound by the Ice King's power.

IV.

The poet sings of the better land,
"Where flowers immortal bloom,"
And so I can partly understand
The glories beyond the tomb;
How sad and dreary this earth would be,
Through all of the weary hours,
Had God not given to you and me
The beautiful birds and flowers.

—John H. Yates.

Indoor window gardens provide an opportunity to create a warm and welcoming atmosphere in the home—and in 1885 inspired a man to write poetry!

VICK'S ILLUSTRATED MONTHLY MAGAZINE 8, 1885

WINDOW GARDENING

(continued from page 36)

at 40 degrees, exposed and in the shade. . . . And you all know how to save frozen plants; keep them in perfect darkness and don't even look at them for two days. G.S.[2]

Gardeners apparently have always waged war on pesky insects. We might wonder if the plants survived this woman's diligence:

My bathroom is close to my south window; and the other day when I discovered the red spider on some fine Geraniums, into the bath-tub they went, and for about two hours the room was given up to tobacco smoke, followed by a thorough sprinkling of soap-suds, and rinsing in clear, blood-warm water. I shower them every few days, occasionally fill the saucers with hot water and use aqua ammonia very freely. I draw a basin full of quite warm water, make a good lather, and then give them all a good ducking, and rinsing, and they are as happy as they can be. I discovered the pot of Cape Jessamine full of worms, but I gave them a strong dose of ammonia, and not a worm lived to tell the tale. I use street dirt for manure, for liquid manure, guano water; for Begonias, street dirt and sand, and they thrive on it wonderfully. I have one that has bloomed constantly since last June.

Washington, D.C. Marie.[3]

The decorative parlor in the Herman Amberg Preus parsonage in Spring Prairie showcases the refined taste of the lady of the house and provides a wonderful location for her precious houseplants and household treasures, circa 1871.
WHI IMAGE ID 27218

NOTES

1. "Subscription Terms, 1877," *The Ladies' Floral Cabinet and Pictorial Companion* (New York: Henry T. Williams, October 1877), 151.

2. "How to Have Plenty of Flowers in Winter," *The Ladies' Floral Cabinet and Pictorial Companion* (New York: Henry T. Williams, January 1875), 2.

3. "Window Gardening," *The Ladies' Floral Cabinet and Pictorial Companion* (New York: Henry T. Williams, January 1875), 6.

Flaunting flowers for only part of the season, perennial blooming plants were relegated to the side or back of the house. These irises and pinks are enjoyed outside the kitchen door at Old World Wisconsin's restored Wesley and Sophia Benson home.
TERRY MOLTER

parents, a common practice after a daughter lost her husband. Emma and her mother ran the household, looked after Charlie, and enjoyed church and social activities.[11]

The Benson home was moved from Fort Atkinson to Old World Wisconsin in 1982 and restored to its 1875 appearance. This middle-class workingman's home features a well-manicured grass lawn, separate flower beds, and a small backyard kitchen garden—all elements typical of a village Yankee home landscape in post–Civil War Wisconsin.

Yankee Recipes

Previous page:
A medley of vegetables from a nineteenth-century kitchen garden
VICK'S FLOWER AND VEGETABLE GARDEN, 1882

Root vegetables on the porch before their trip to the kitchen; from left to right: assorted turnips, rutabagas, and parsnips
NANCY L. KLEMP

Real New England Brown Bread

This popular Yankee recipe from *Wisconsin & Iowa Farmer, and Northwestern Cultivator* (1855) is remarkably similar to Sarah Josepha Hale's recipe for rye and Indian bread in *The Good Housekeeper*, published in 1841. She writes, "This is a sweet and nourishing diet, and generally acceptable to children."[1]

Indian meal and cornmeal are one and the same. A gill equals one-fourth of an imperial pint, or five fluid ounces.

Take equal proportions of sifted rye and Indian meal, mix them well together; add half a teacupfull of molasses, and two gills of good yeast to about three quarts of the mixed meal. Wet this with good, new milk, sufficient to make a dough that can easily be worked, even with one hand. For economy's sake, milk that has stood twelve hours and from which the cream has been taken, may be a substitute for the new milk; or water which has been pressed from boiled squash, or in which squash has been boiled, is a substitute much better than pure water. But warm water is more commonly used. The ingredients should be thoroughly mixed, and stand, in cold weather, for twelve hours; in warm weather two hours may be sufficient before baking.

If baked in a brick oven, a three-quart loaf should stand in the oven all night. The same quantity in three baking pans will bake in about three hours.

Serve this warm from the oven with good, sweet butter, and we could *feast* upon it every morning for breakfast, from January to December.[2]

Beans for Soup

Easily grown, dried, and stored for year-round use, many varieties of beans were planted in nineteenth-century American gardens and were staples in home kitchens. Beans provided healthful, filling fare hearty enough to be used in place of meat, if necessary. This 1855 recipe is perfect for the family on a tight budget. Be sure to soak the beans overnight before proceeding.

To provide an excellent dinner—healthful, palatable and nutritious—take a pint of beans, with one gallon of water, and the beef bones we are accustomed to throw in the street. Boil all together (adding a few potatoes, if convenient) until the beans become soft—add salt and pepper to suit the taste, and the dinner is ready. Such a dinner costs next to nothing; and will rest easier upon the stomach than venison steaks, quail or partridge, washed down with champagne.

A piece of fat beef thrown into the pot, will give a pretty good flavor to soupe porridge, or such a dish as I have named. But if you want the genuine flavor, use bones, such bones as are usually thrown away. There is a flavor obtained from the bones which is not given from solid meat.—*N.Y. Journal of Commerce*[3]

Turnips Stewed in Butter

Every nineteenth-century kitchen garden included turnips. The 1872 *B. K. Bliss and Son's Illustrated Spring Catalogue and Amateurs Guide to the Flower and Kitchen Garden* listed fifteen varieties! The Yankees enjoyed their vegetables well cooked and, in this case, stewed in plenty of butter.

This is an excellent way of dressing the vegetable when it is mild and finely grained, but its flavor otherwise is too strong to be agreeable. After they have been washed, wiped quite dry, and pared, slice the turnips nearly half an inch thick, and divide them into halves. Just dissolve an ounce of butter for each half slice of the turnips, put them in as flat as they can be, and stew them very gently indeed, from three-quarters of an hour to a full hour. Add a seasoning of salt and white pepper when they are half done. When thus prepared, they may be dished over fried or nicely broiled mutton cutlets, or served by themselves.[4]

Potato Pudding

Potatoes, in one form or another, graced every table—and frequently more than once a day. Always looking for new ways to prepare the familiar staple, Midwestern housewives no doubt were delighted to try this recipe when they saw it in *Wisconsin & Iowa Farmer, and Northwestern Cultivator* in 1855.

Boil three large mealy potatoes, mash them very smoothly and put in one ounce of butter and two or three table-spoonsful of thick cream; then add three well beaten eggs, a little salt, grated nutmeg, and a table-spoonful of brown sugar. Beat all well together, and bake in a buttered dish for half or three-quarters of an hour.[5]

Salsify, or Vegetable Oysters

Oysters and salsify (or vegetable oysters) enjoyed great popularity in the nineteenth century. Salsify, easily grown in the garden, has a taste slightly reminiscent of the oyster. If the cook was able to prepare the root vegetable in a manner so it also had the proper oyster appearance, so much the better.

Wash the roots perfectly clean and drop them into boiling water; when done, take up and mash; add sweet milk and flour sufficient to bake a batter. Season with salt and pepper and such other condiments as the oyster requires, and fry in butter. Another way in which they are very delicious is, to grate the root on as fine a grater as it will pass through; add sweet milk, just enough to cover it, and boil; when done, add flour enough to make a batter; season with salt and pepper; break two or three eggs in and stir the whole together; fry in butter or very sweet lard, and the resemblance to oysters is complete.[6]

Spinach

To say the Yankees prepared their vegetables well cooked might be an understatement. Suspicious of food in the raw state, the woman who prepared this dish could rest assured she had cooked the greens thoroughly to guard her family's health (think green mush on toast!).

This is one of the most delicious of the whole tribe of the greens family. Wash the leaves carefully and drop them into boiling water, in which there has been a little salt put; ten or fifteen minutes will be enough to cook them. When done, take up and drain through a cullender. Now season with butter, pepper and salt, and lay over some slices of toasted bread and serve up for the table.[7]

The leaves of Swiss chard—also known as sea kale beet, leaf beet, or silver beet—may be substituted for spinach leaves. The Swiss chard stalks may be prepared and eaten like asparagus. Only the aboveground parts of this beet species are used.
NANCY L. KLEMP

Young seedpods of the Rat-Tail radish are delicious raw or pickled. Some Yankees even boiled them to serve as cooked vegetables.
NANCY L. KLEMP

To Pickle Radish Pods

Many early Wisconsinites grew radishes. The delightful Rat-Tail radish flowers profusely and then produces the thin pods for which this variety is grown. The crunchy, mildly radish-flavored pods may be added to salad or pickled—a tasty snack.

Cut them in nice bunches as soon as they are fully formed; they must be young and tender; pour boiling salt and water on them, cover with a thick cloth and pewter plate, to keep in the steam; repeat this every day till they are a good green, then put them in cold vinegar, with mace and white pepper; mix a little turmeric with a small portion of oil, and stir it into the vinegar; it will make the pods of a more lively green. They are very pretty for garnishing meats.[8]

Bird's Nest

The traditional cooked fruit with custard sauce was baked in one dish and made an attractive presentation. A "quick" or hot oven referred to how fast the oven was burning and was equivalent to 400 degrees.

Pare six or eight large apples (Spitzenbergs or Greenings are best), and remove the core by cutting from the end down into the middle, so as to leave the apple whole except where the core has been removed; place them as near together as they can stand with the open part upward in a deep pie-dish; next make a thin batter, using one quart sweet milk, three eggs with sufficient flour, and pour it into the dish around the apples, also filling the cavities in them; bake them in a quick oven; eat them with butter and sugar.[9]

Popcorn

Popcorn has long been enjoyed as a popular snack. Grown with other field crops, families welcomed it to the kitchen where, in 1853, the recommended preparation involved deep-frying in lard. No pan shaking is required, but remember to remove and drain the popped kernels.

Not one in a hundred of those who are so fond of popcorn, know how to pop it. It is a simple process, attended with very little labor, and a rich, tender, luscious dish is prepared, that Queen Vic, or Pope Pius probably, within all their splendor, know nothing about.

Lard is to be heated in the same manner as for frying "doughnuts," and half a pint, or such a matter, of the "eight row, tucket corn" is to be thrown in, and covered immediately to prevent the kernels from flying out on to the floor. In an instant a pop, pop, popping will commence—such as you never heard before. A minute after the popping ceases take off the cover, and dip out with a skimmer, draining off the grease, and turn into a sieve, put upon a pan, to drain. The pan should be kept upon a stove, so that the corn will retain its heat long enough for the lard to run off, otherwise it will be too greasy. While cooling, salt to your taste.[10]

Squash Pie

Yankees readily adapted New World crops into their menus. Any mature winter squash or pumpkin could be used for a delicious pie, although squash traditionally received a more enthusiastic response. "The Pumpkin is now but little used, except for agricultural purposes, the Squashes being so much sweeter and drier and finely grained. No good gardener, we think, would tolerate a pumpkin in the garden, nor would any sensible cook allow one in the kitchen." Yet "some persons will always defend the good old-fashioned pumpkin pie, against all innovators."[11]

Pare, take out the seeds, and stew the squash till very soft and dry. Strain or rub it through a sieve or colander. Mix this with good milk till it is as thick as batter; sweeten it with sugar. Allow five eggs to a quart of milk, beat the eggs well, add them to the squash, and season with rose-water, cinnamon, nutmeg, or whatever spices you like. Line a pie-plate with crust, fill and bake about an hour.[12]

The Cushaw squash or pumpkin may be harvested young for use as a summer squash. Allowed to mature fully, it becomes a nice winter squash. Happily, this heirloom variety is not attractive to the squash vine borer.

NANCY L. KLEMP

GERMAN SETTLER GARDENS

Grapes were eaten fresh at the table or made into jam, jelly, juice, or wine. Germans exhibited great skill at making wine.
NANCY L. KLEMP

selection of plants. The plans for an ideal monastery garden, which date to 816 and are preserved at the Abbey of St. Gall near the Swiss-German border today, show a garden layout of tidy, symmetrical, rectangular beds of plants surrounded on four sides by a wall. In 795 Charlemagne, the first Holy Roman emperor, issued a decree that included a list of plants to be grown in the imperial gardens throughout his empire. Many of the seventy-three vegetables, herbs, and flowers named continued to be grown in German kitchen gardens more than one thousand years later.

Typically situated with a southern or eastern exposure, the garden took advantage of available sunlight. Conveniently located right next to the house, it sometimes filled the entire front yard. The garden was laid out in rectangular beds, with straight paths dividing it into a geometric pattern. Sometimes two intersecting paths split the garden into quadrants; often it was further divided by straight secondary paths, creating an orderly checkerboard effect. Pathways were covered with any local material—available free for the taking or at little expense—to avoid tracking mud into the house. Common choices included gravel, sand, tanner's bark (tannin removed from tree bark was used in treating animal skins to make leather; the leftover bark was readily available from area tanneries), or wooden boards laid down to form a boardwalk. Edgings of low-growing plants sometimes further defined individual beds, whether level with the ground or raised. When improved soil drainage was desirable, raised beds benefited plant growth. Not merely a collection of vegetables, the German-American kitchen garden enjoyed a happy mix of vegetables, herbs, and flowers, often within the same bed.

A well or a barrel to collect rainwater often resided within the garden, as did a bench or seat from which the garden could be admired.[1] Typically, plants or paths covered every bit of ground, and a fence made of inexpensive or, even better, "found" locally available material such as branches, cut and woven between wooden posts, surrounded the entire garden (a great use for buckthorn).

A specially selected tree—frequently a walnut, pear, cherry, or linden—was designated as the protector of the house and traditionally grew near the dwelling. As with all trees, it grew outside the kitchen garden enclosure so as not to shade or disturb the plants.

Opposite page:
A happy mix of vegetables, herbs, and flowers. A bench on which to sit and admire the garden calls from the porch.
GERALD H. EMMERICH JR.

Well-manicured geometric garden beds at the Charles and Auguste Schulz House. Note the top of the woven fence in the foreground.
GERALD H. EMMERICH JR.

Germans in their fatherland considered one hundred square yards (nine hundred square feet) *per family member* an ideal size for a kitchen garden, although between one hundred and three hundred square yards (nine hundred to twenty-seven hundred square feet) *per family* was probably the norm.[2] With more land available, gardens in America tended to be even larger. Potatoes and cabbage, basic ingredients in the family diet, grew with the field crops rather than in the kitchen garden and are not included in these dimensions. The one hundred heads of cabbage typically planted *per family member* and plenty of potatoes (enough to eat in season plus at least twenty-five bushels to store for the family's winter use) required considerable growing space.

Wisconsin Germans devised ingenious and effective storage methods to keep the great quantities of produce desired to sustain the family through to the next growing season. Pickling and brining were popular methods of food preservation, and much of the white cabbage became sauerkraut. Families filled their root cellars with vegetables and went on to store produce in barrels buried in the ground. They dug trenches and pits and even mounded the garden's bounty aboveground and then covered the produce to protect it from rain and winter weather. Coverings often included layers of straw, pea and potato vines, or dug turf turned root-side-up and topped off with pine boughs

Early German immigrants thought lettuce produced a mild narcotic effect, helpful in the treatment of pain and sleeplessness. Lettuce juice was said to be effective against a hangover.
SIGNE EMMERICH

Opposite page:
A simple fence woven of branches allows light and breezes to pass through the garden while providing protection from roaming animals.
LOYD HEATH

or soil. During the bitterest cold temperatures, horse manure was piled on top, generating additional warmth and protection.[3]

Germans enjoyed their vegetables and considered them important for good health. Healing properties for specific ailments were even attributed to numerous vegetables. Turnip juice was used to treat chicken pox.[4] Scorzonera or black salsify was thought to be an effective treatment for lung infections; drinking the liquid in which it was cooked reputedly helped clear the lungs and aid breathing. Consumed regularly, celeriac was thought to relieve rheumatism.[5] Whether eaten raw, cooked, pickled, or prepared with sweet-and-sour flavoring, homegrown vegetables were grown in large quantities and great variety by German-Americans in Wisconsin.

Fruit also added to the diversity of the German-American diet and was enjoyed fresh or dried; in jams, jellies, and syrups; in baked goods; and in juice or wine. Gooseberries as well as red and black currants traveled from the Old Country to be planted in Wisconsin kitchen gardens. Apple trees thrived, and varieties of grapes native to America quickly replaced failed European varieties so German immigrants could continue their traditions of making wine and eating fresh grapes. Hickory nuts, walnuts, elderberries, and raspberries gathered from the wild offered additional culinary variety without using valuable garden space.

This page and opposite: Noted for their beauty and brilliancy, zinnias were among the colorful annual flowers enjoyed in nineteenth-century German-American gardens.
MIKE MORBECK

Herbs in the kitchen garden were sources of homegrown medicine and insect repellents, provided wonderful flavoring and fragrance, and could be crafted into decorations to meet the housewife's needs and pleasures. Early German settlers also grew dye plants to color homegrown wool and linen. One example was woad, an ancient plant whose leaves yielded blue dye and which also brought visual delight to the garden in springtime when it grew four feet tall with masses of brilliant sunshine-yellow flowers.

Many varieties of well-loved flowers planted in the kitchen garden brought joy to the family with their beauty and fragrance. Imagine precise rectangles filled with deep-red leafy beet tops, quilted gray-green savoy cabbages, spiky leeks and onions, ferny-topped carrots, tender corn salad, multicolored lettuces, shining Swiss chard, wavy-edged endive, cheerful orange and yellow nasturtiums trying to escape their straight-edged confines, robust marshmallow, pastel asters, mop-headed peonies, charming sweet pinks and sweet Williams, happy zinnias, fragrant sweet marjoram, summer savory and thyme, refreshingly pungent peppermint, aromatic lavender, and dreamy roses in shades of pink and white, all woven together to create a stunning living geometric patchwork quilt.

Neat and orderly, well tended and filled with a wide variety of colors, textures, fragrances, and flavors, the beauty and diversity of the German-American kitchen gardens set them distinctly apart from their neighbors. Each kitchen garden expressed its owner's individuality. Although they shared many common characteristics, no two gardens were ever identical.

Bull's Blood beets bring vivid color to the garden and table; both leaves and roots are used in the kitchen. Embracing the spirit of German frugality, Old World Wisconsin gardeners cover pathways with sawdust—material freely available from an on-site steam-powered sawmill.
TERRY MOLTER

Space was rarely wasted on lawns of grass in the early years of German-American settlement. Such a useless luxury produced nothing for the household yet required frequent cutting. However, sometimes an area of sturdy grasses occasionally brightened with daisies grew near the side or back of the house. Clothes could be laid to dry and linens could bleach in the sun in this area known as the *bleiche*, from the German *bleichen*, meaning "to bleach."

A fine example of the early German-American immigrants who settled in Wisconsin is Charles August Schulz. With his wife, Auguste, and their five children, Schulz left Pomerania for bustling Watertown in south-central Wisconsin in 1856. (Pomerania, located on the Baltic coast, was one of a number of independent states that joined together in 1871 to become the Unified States of Germany.) By 1860 the Schulz family had grown to include eight children. They owned and lived on 154 acres of farmland, which included 60 acres under cultivation, in the nearby Town of Herman in Dodge County.

The Schulz farm raised wheat, a lucrative cash crop in 1860, as well as smaller quantities of oats, rye, grass seed, hay, and potatoes. In the German tradition, the

Schulzes saw to the needs of the family first and then raised crops and products to sell. Rye especially pleased housewives, who baked the popular round loaves of dark German rye bread with flour from the ground grain. Wasting nothing, the Germans sold the rye straw for the manufacture of horse collars. The Schulzes raised a quarter acre of flax from which they processed and wove linen. After saving some of the seed for planting future crops, they took the remaining flaxseed to a nearby oil mill to be pressed for linseed oil, another source of income.[6] The oil was used primarily in the manufacturing of paint and varnish. The Schulzes raised sheep, sold wool, raised cows, and made and sold butter. Living in an area with an abundance of maple trees, they processed and sold maple sugar and molasses.[7] Good German farmers saw the potential for additional income at every turn and let few opportunities slip by.

Auguste Schulz's responsibilities centered on the needs of the house and the family, and she no doubt devoted considerable time to the maintenance of her large kitchen garden. Created within a tightly knit Pomeranian community, her family garden in 1860 surely followed the traditional pattern of planting in orderly geometric beds. Madder, woad, and tansy—dye plants to color wool and linen in shades of red, blue, green, and gold—shared space with other long-familiar plants. Also popular were scorzonera (or black salsify) and savoy cabbage, rarely seen outside German gardens in the nineteenth century.

Relocated to Old World Wisconsin in 1975, the Charles and Auguste Schulz home was painstakingly restored to its 1860 appearance. A kitchen garden has been re-created based on extensive research of nineteenth-century gardening practices of German immigrants in Wisconsin as well as of traditions in their fatherland. Lush combinations of flowers, vegetables, and herbs fill the front yard *bauergarten*, offering a treat for the senses. Present-day gardeners can appreciate the pride and satisfaction Auguste, a dedicated German-American farmwife, must have felt when she paused to admire the kitchen garden she so lovingly created and so diligently tended for the nourishment of the bodies and spirits of her family members.

4 Roots of Change

Wisconsin's German population grew through the late nineteenth century, as immigration continued and families and ethnically cohesive communities increased in numbers. Fine schools, where lessons often were taught in German, ensured a quality education. Adults enjoyed numerous social activities within their communities, including participation in horticultural societies and garden clubs.

While maintaining many of their own ethnic customs, German-Americans continuously sought to improve their lot and to work more efficiently and frugally. Not being great risk takers, their progress in adopting American advances in farm technology and machinery tended to be slow but steady. When introduced to laborsaving devices or progressive agricultural ideas or practices, they proved willing to adapt and change—if they considered the change to be prudent.

By 1880, the family kitchen garden showed evidence of the influences of mainstream America. Once center stage and a showpiece to the onlooker, the kitchen garden found itself relegated to the side yard, still enclosed by a fence but separated from the house. The German tradition of mingling flowers and herbs with vegetables continued, but plantings in neat rows replaced the traditional rectangular beds, allowing for mechanical cultivation, if desired.

Imagine row after row of fine vegetables and flowers, all neatly lined up and cleanly cultivated, sprinkled with fragrant herbs. Newer varieties of vegetables replaced the old in

Perennial strawberry plants edge the boardwalk path, and rhubarb is visible in the foreground on the right. Both overwinter in the ground. Beyond the kitchen garden fence, the south side of the picturesque *fachwerk* or half-timber home of the Friedrich and Sophia Koepsell Farm is visible. The house was relocated from the Town of Jackson, Washington County, to Old World Wisconsin and restored to its circa 1880 appearance.
NANCY L. KLEMP

By 1880 many Wisconsin Germans had abandoned the custom from their homeland of planting kitchen gardens in beds in favor of the American style of planting in rows. One tradition German immigrants retained was raising hops to brew beer. Poles for hops vines to climb stand just inside the fence; an apple orchard is visible beyond.
SIGNE EMMERICH

many instances, and New World plants joined old familiar friends. Rhubarb, winter squash, and even tomatoes became part of the culinary mix. Handsome chrysanthemums, wavy-edged petunias, and stunning dahlias flaunted themselves among the flowers.

Fewer medicinal herbs took space in the garden, and dye plants disappeared altogether, no longer deemed important as patent medicines and synthetic dyes became available, affordable, and more widely accepted.

Currants, gooseberries, strawberries, asparagus, and other hardy perennial vegetables, flowers, and herbs grew as borders or in their own sections of the garden to remain undisturbed while dormant over winter months. Liberally manured, lovingly tended, and still the pride of the housewife, the orderly and attractive kitchen garden continued to supply much of the family's basic needs.

Pumpkins grew with the field crops, as did great quantities of potatoes and cabbages, and often beans and peas as well. Most farms also maintained an orchard of apple trees.

German immigrants valued practicality and efficiency. Visitors at the Koepsell home have a direct route out of the back door from the kitchen, across the porch, along the boardwalk to the gate, through the garden, and straight into the privy. The fruit press at the end of the porch offered the farm family an efficient means of processing fruit for juice, jelly, or wine.
GERALD. H. EMMERICH JR.

THE WHEEL HOE

The wheel hoe was a hand-pushed garden cultivator. The simplest models consisted of a single wheel, double handle, and cultivating tooth or plow attachment. In theory, the wheel hoe eliminated the backbreaking work of hand-hoeing. In reality, after the cultivator passed down rows between growing plants, two narrow sidebands of unworked soil remained in need of hoeing by hand. The wheel hoe's overall effectiveness as a weeding tool, however, was good enough to inspire improvements in design.

By the 1880s American manufacturers were producing wheel hoes at an impressive rate, evidenced by how many companies made them and by their steady appearance in seed and hardware company catalogs. An 1876 advertisement in *D. M. Ferry & Co.'s Catalogue of Garden, Flower and Agricultural Seeds* described Holbrook's New Hand Cultivator as "much improved for 1876. . . . The rear teeth have side-guards, to allow them to work within half an inch of plants and save nearly all the hand weeding."[1] The wheel hoe's growth in popularity was related to its growing versatility. The Comstock Hand Cultivator and Onion Weeder combined two adjustable rake heads with three cultivator attachments and company advertisements made the claim that it "will do the work of SIX MEN with hoes."[2]

Before the close of the nineteenth century, wheel hoe manufacturers successfully incorporated the work of the cultivator, plow, seeder, hoe, rake, and garden marker in one remarkable implement for use by the home gardener. The most widely recognized of these multiuse tools was the "Planet Jr." brand. Well into the 1930s, Planet Jr. double- and single-wheel hoes, seed drills, rakes, plows, and any combination thereof populated American gardens. For decades, the reasonably priced, high-quality Planet Jr. models were retailed through Montgomery Ward & Company and the Sears, Roebuck catalogs—another winning combination.

Holbrook's New Hand Cultivator, recommended for use in small gardens of one to five acres, was one of many styles of wheel hoes manufactured in America during the last quarter of the nineteenth century.

D. M. FERRY & CO.'S CATALOGUE OF GARDEN, FLOWER AND AGRICULTURAL SEEDS, 1876

THE WHEEL HOE

A reproduction Planet Jr. cultivator in action. TERRY MOLTER

It is interesting to note that the "modern" wheel hoe, purported to be a wonderful laborsaving device in the garden—perfect for quick and clean cultivation between rows—was slow to gain acceptance by Wisconsin Germans.[3] Eternally frugal, they rarely spent money unnecessarily. Personal labor was assessed no value, and homemade tools sufficed in the garden. Ideally, any materials and supplies needed could be found locally, with little or no cash outlay.

NOTES

1. *D. M. Ferry & Co.'s Catalogue of Garden, Flower and Agricultural Seeds* (Detroit: O. S. Gulley's Stram Presses, 1876), 230.

2. *B. K. Bliss and Son's Illustrated Spring Catalogue and Amateurs Guide to the Flower and Kitchen Garden* (New York: B. K. Bliss & Son, 1872), 105.

3. James William Miller, "German Heirloom Gardening Research Report" (Old World Wisconsin unpublished manuscript, February 2002), 32.

The front of the restored Friedrich and Sophia Koepsell home. A lawn of grass and a bed of flowers reflect an American influence on the German immigrants' home landscape.
NANCY L. KLEMP

Dahlias and Drummond's phlox bloom in a circular flower bed cut into the lawn.
GERALD H. EMMERICH JR.

Potted myrtles greet visitors. Myrtle held special significance as the herb of love and was traditionally used in weddings and at funerals. These highly valued tender perennials are brought inside for protection over winter.

In 1885 James Vick wrote of myrtle in *Vick's Illustrated Monthly Magazine*: "It seems to be a general favorite with the Germans who grow it to perfection. I know of specimens a dozen years old belonging to German families in this vicinity, and the family cow would be parted with quite as readily as they would part with their Myrtle. I have often tried to buy a fine specimen, but in vain. They will willingly give cuttings of it, or offer to start a plant for you, but 'Nein, nein,' they can't let the old plant go."

NANCY L. KLEMP

Houseplants spend the summer outdoors. From left to right: myrtle, sage, prostrate rosemary, red geranium, Crystal Palace Gem geranium, English ivy, rose geranium, Crystal Palace Gem and red geraniums, and prostrate rosemary.

SIGNE EMMERICH

HOTBEDS AND COLD FRAMES 

Gardeners wanting an early harvest or to jump-start the growth of vegetables that take a full season to mature build a hotbed—a place to sow seeds six to eight weeks before transplanting in the garden. Always positioned facing south and ideally sheltered from northerly winds by a building or fence line, hotbeds are bottomless wooden frames topped with a lattice of glass window panes called sashing. Enclosed within or below the frame is a deep bed of horse dung and straw. Heat is generated as the organic materials slowly ferment. Once warmed by the fermentation process, the bed is topped with several inches of rich soil and is then ready to be sown.

The rarified environment of the hotbed frame requires meticulous care. Every day a bit of fresh air is introduced by raising the sashes. On warm days the windows might be completely removed to prevent plants from scalding in the rising steam. In 1843, an issue of *The Gardener's Manual* cautioned its readers that maintenance of a hotbed "requires you to be thoughtful and regular."[1] The author recommended building a hotbed—if not for the benefit of a large garden, then simply to promote good habits through discipline. Associating attentive and thrifty gardening practice with improvement in character was not uncommon among gardening enthusiasts writing for the common classes.

A cold frame is similar to a hotbed but is not built on a base of manure and straw; it rests instead on open ground. Window sashing on the cold frame similarly helps retain moisture but without the added heat generated by a fermenting mixture of

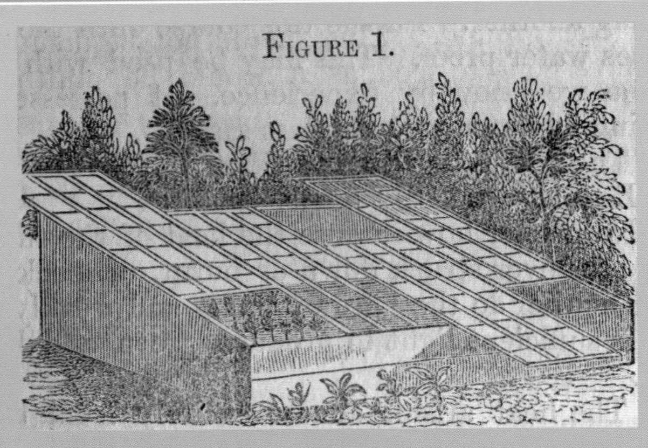

This illustration of a standard hotbed frame shows how the sash is designed to slide up or down to control moisture levels inside the frame. The same reference describes a "German Hot Bed" similarly built but using waterproof cloth in place of sash glass. Mention of this economical alternative includes directions for waterproofing a plain cotton cloth. It required repeated applications of a mixture comprised of lime water, linseed oil, egg whites, and egg yolks.

E. M. TUBBS, *THE NEW HAMPSHIRE KITCHEN, FRUIT, AND FLORAL GARDENER* (PETERBORO, NH: K. C. SCOTT, 1852)

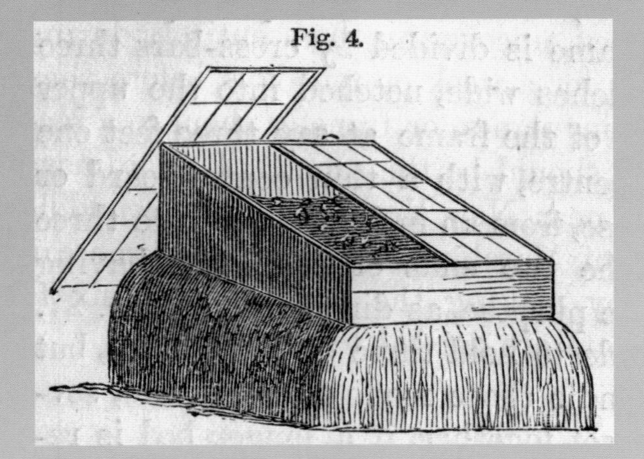

Hotbed frames can be built atop a bedding of manure and straw, as in this illustration, or the bedding can be enclosed within the frame.

ALEXANDER WATSON, *THE AMERICAN HOME GARDEN*

HOTBEDS AND COLD FRAMES

A microclimate is created by the use of a bell-glass over potted plants, shown on the left. The glass dome traps moist air, thereby reducing soil evaporation. This greenhouse effect strengthens maturing root systems. On the right, an ordinary household goblet is upturned and set upon a pot, achieving the same effect.

VICK'S ILLUSTRATED MONTHLY MAGAZINE 2, 1879

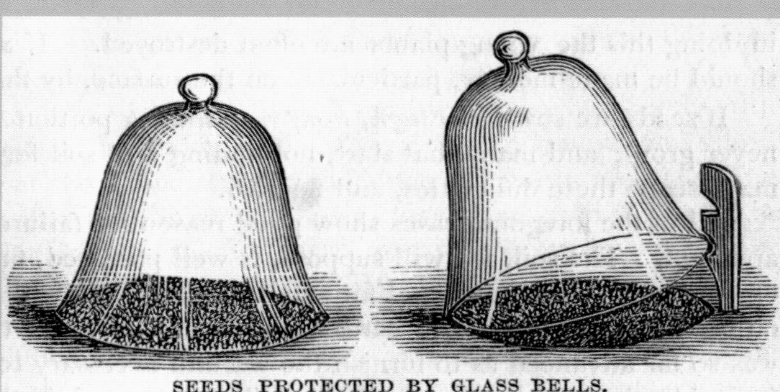

SEEDS PROTECTED BY GLASS BELLS.

Placed over freshly sown seeds, the bell-glass hastens germination and then offers protection to newly hatched seedlings. The bell-glass on the right is tipped to provide ventilation, allowing excess heat and moisture to escape, and encouraging strong plant growth as air moves over the young seedlings.

VICK'S FLOWER AND VEGETABLE GARDEN, 1876

manure and straw. For young plants reared in the warmth of the hotbed, a stop in the cold frame before being transplanted in the garden offers time for adjustment and hardening.

A bell-glass is like a portable cold frame. These bell-shaped, blown-glass domes are placed over newly sown seeds or individual young plants. Whether an overturned glass tumbler or goblet is used to cover plants in a pot or the more formal bell-glass or bell-jar is placed over pots or young plants in the garden, the effect is the same: a moist environment in which to hasten seed germination and secure the early growth of young cuttings. An added benefit is the charming appearance of the bell-glass itself.

NOTE

1. *The Gardener's Manual* (New York: The United Society, 1843), 10.

By 1880 American influence was already in evidence as the front yards of many rural German-American homes were converted to lawns of grass (how utterly useless and totally extravagant!) decorated with beds devoted entirely to flowers. An 1881 history of Washington and Ozaukee counties noted, "As is characteristic with the Germans, most of them have elegant yards decorated with neatly arranged walks and flower beds."[1]

Productive and beautiful, the fields and gardens of nineteenth-century Wisconsin Germans received well-deserved admiration from those who saw them.

Friedrich Koepsell, his wife, Sophia, and their three children emigrated from Pomerania to Washington County in southeastern Wisconsin in 1857 and settled near an established German community. A skilled carpenter and house builder, Koepsell soon purchased forty acres and built a large and fine half-timber home for his family in the nearby Town of Jackson. The family grew to include nine children, and by 1880 five of them lived at home. Koepsell continued his carpentry business and also ran a diversified farm, probably with the help of his sons, that included a home dairy; a mix of additional farm animals including a few horses, sheep, pigs, and chickens; and a variety of crops. Twenty-four acres planted to grain included wheat and barley for cash crops, with the barley purchased by local brewers for beer making. Corn and oats were sold for livestock feed, and the rye was ground for flour.[2] Beyond their kitchen garden, which provided much of the family's nourishment, the Koepsells grew an acre of potatoes and devoted a half acre to apple trees.

At Old World Wisconsin's 1880 Friedrich and Sophia Koepsell Farm restoration, the garden is located off to the side of the house, situated to the south to take advantage of the available sunlight. A fine boardwalk, two and one-half feet wide—a natural choice for a carpenter accustomed to working with wood—offers a direct route from the back porch to a garden gate, through the garden, and straight into an attractive wooden privy. The latter being a popular destination, opportunities abound for visitors to admire a well-tended garden enclosed with an unpainted picket fence, just as folks did well over 100 years ago. Orderly rows of produce are easily accessible from the boardwalk and quite convenient to the kitchen, located just inside the back porch door.

A large front lawn of grass and a fashionably modern "American"-style flower bed cut into that lawn show evidence of a Wisconsin German family's assimilation of influences from outside their own community.

The entrance to a German-American kitchen garden, circa 1880, re-created at Old World Wisconsin's Friedrich and Sophia Koepsell Farm
GERALD H. EMMERICH JR.

Apple trees such as these at the Koepsell Farm grew on most nineteenth-century German farms in Wisconsin. Sometimes the fruit was cooked with vegetables for a bit of culinary excitement.
NANCY L. KLEMP

German Recipes

Previous page:
Beans in their pods await shelling and share the company of assorted vegetables and fruits.
GERALD H. EMMERICH JR.

Opposite page:
Any herbs not used fresh were often hung to dry for winter use. Inside the bake house or summer kitchen of Old World Wisconsin's 1875 German Schottler Farm, a cloth has been threaded to catch dried dill seed to use for flavoring or to save for next season's planting.
TERRY MOLTER

Herb Soup *(Kräutersuppe)*

This flavorful and aromatic soup made use of the fresh herbs and leafy greens so abundantly grown in German-American gardens.

Take a handful of sorrel, purslane, basil, lettuce, spinach, tarragon, burnet, chives, or whatever appropriate herbs you have—though not too much of the stronger flavored ones—and wash them thoroughly and cut them up fine. Melt a big piece of butter and add as much flour as is needed for a soup, then add the herbs and some soup stock. Then flavor with chervil, parsley, and salt. Thicken the soup with egg yolks and then add potatoes or egg dumplings.[1]

Rye Bread

The dough for traditional round loaves of dark German rye bread was placed in round rye straw baskets and set in a warm place to rise. After the second rising, the loaves were placed on a wooden board and slid into the bake oven, where they baked until done.

2 ounces yeast in ¼ cup warm water
1 pint milk
¼ cup molasses
3 tablespoons butter
about 5 to 7 cups rye flour
1 teaspoon salt

Dissolve yeast in warm water. Scald milk; cool to lukewarm. Combine molasses and butter in bowl. Add dissolved yeast and milk, enough flour to make a soft dough, and salt. Knead until elastic. Place in rye straw baskets (or a greased bowl). Cover with cloth and place in black kitchen[2] near oven for about 2 hours to rise. Punch down, divide dough, and shape into loaves. Let rise again for about 1 hour. Bake until done.[3]

A tasty turnip assortment, left to right: White Egg, Purple Top White Globe, and Amber Globe
NANCY L. KLEMP

While common green cabbage was relegated to grow with field crops, red cabbage enjoyed a place in the German-American kitchen garden.
SANDRA MATSON

Turnip and Potato Whip

Potatoes and turnips appeared frequently in the garden and on the table. They join flavors in this simple and popular recipe.

3 cups peeled and cubed turnips
3 cups peeled and cubed potatoes
2 tablespoons chopped onion
2 tablespoons butter
salt and pepper, to taste
hot milk or cream

Cook turnips, potatoes, and onion in salted water until tender. Drain and dry. Mash quickly together with butter and seasoning, add hot milk, and cream until fluffy.[4]

Red Cabbage

This sweet-and-sour cabbage recipe showcases a time-honored favorite combination of flavors among Germans.

1 large red cabbage
3 tablespoons bacon drippings
1 onion, chopped
2 apples, peeled and diced
½ cup vinegar
1 tablespoon white sugar
1 teaspoon salt
1 bay leaf
½ cup red currant jelly

Slice cabbage with large slicer or knife. Rinse and drain well. Heat bacon drippings in a large kettle and saute the chopped onion until it is transparent. Add cabbage and cook about 10 minutes. Stir frequently until cabbage begins to wilt. Add apples, vinegar, sugar, salt, and bay leaf. Mix, cover, and simmer 2 hours on back of stove, stirring from time to time. Add jelly, stirring until it is melted and well blended. Move pan to front of stove and bring to a boil. Return to back of stove, cover, and simmer 10 minutes.[5]

Black Salsify Salad *(Schwarzwurzelsalat)*

Rarely grown outside German gardens, scorzonera, or black salsify, is a fine root vegetable. The washed and peeled roots are best cooked in a nonmetal pot, in water with a little vinegar or milk added to help preserve their white color.

Take good, not too thick roots, wash, peel, and cook them in salt water with a little vinegar until they are soft. Drain and put on a towel to dry. In the meantime take six hard-boiled egg yolks, and put them through a fine sieve, then add salt, a half teaspoon each of sugar and pepper, and then add oil, some good vinegar and a tablespoon of blanched, finely chopped parsley to make a good thick sauce. Pour the sauce over the salsify and serve. You can garnish the salad with some small, blanched Brussels sprouts if you like.[6]

Potatoes provided basic nineteenth-century sustenance for German immigrants and were often served at every meal.
TERRY MOLTER

Opposite page:
Cooking on a woodstove at Old World Wisconsin's 1880 German Koepsell Farm
TERRY MOLTER

Potatoes with Apples *(Kartoffeln mit Äpfel)*

As Germans sometimes ate potatoes three times a day, many homegrown combinations appeared at mealtime; some included vegetables with fruit. Potatoes with apples became a favorite.

Cook the potatoes for a little, and then pour off the water and then replace with fresh boiling water. Cook until half done. Add about half as many washed, peeled, cored, and quartered sour apples. If the apples are very sour, add some sugar. Once both are done, mash them and then add lots of pork fat, along with some fried bacon.[7]

U.S. Patent'd March 8. 1879.
Canada Pat'd. April 26 1879.

Blindes Huhn

The origin of the name *blindes huhn* is unknown, but this vegetables with apples and bacon medley is an old recipe that continues to be well received.

4 large carrots, scraped and cubed
½ pound green beans, broken in pieces
3 slices bacon
1 to 2 onions, sliced
2 to 3 apples, peeled and sliced
1 tablespoon sugar
2 tablespoons vinegar
salt, to taste

Cook carrots and beans in salted water until almost tender; drain; saute bacon until crisp; remove from pan, drain, and crumble. Cook onions in bacon fat until soft but not brown. Add apples, sugar, vinegar, and the partially cooked carrots and beans. Replace bacon and add salt. Cook mixture, covered, until vegetables are tender.[8]

Attractive to view and delicious to eat, *blindes huhn*, which translates to "blind hen," contains no hint of chicken flavor.
SANDRA MATSON

Onion Pie *(Zwiebelkuchen)*

***Zwiebelkuchen* translates to "onion cake." This recipe is similar to modern-day quiche, but the caraway seeds add a distinctively German flavor.**

PASTRY:

2 cups flour
1 teaspoon baking powder
½ teaspoon salt
¾ cup butter
1 medium egg, beaten
1 tablespoon cream (optional)
1 egg white, unbeaten

Combine the flour, baking powder, and salt. Chop in the butter and work the mixture with your fingers until it is mealy. Add the egg; blend in the egg until the mixture is the consistency of pie dough. Add the cream if the dough is not sufficiently moist. Working lightly, pat the dough into the bottom and sides of a 9-inch round cake pan. Brush the egg white over the bottom crust to prevent the crust from becoming soggy.

FILLING:

2 cups chopped onions
2 slices bacon, diced
2 tablespoons butter
¼ teaspoon salt
1 teaspoon caraway seeds
½ tablespoon flour
½ cup heavy cream
2 medium eggs, beaten

Cook the onions and bacon in butter until they are very soft. Add the salt and caraway seeds. Blend in the flour, then slowly add the cream. Remove the ingredients from the heat. Add a little of the mixture to the beaten eggs, then combine the two. Spoon the mixture into the pastry-lined pan. Bake at 375 degrees until the pastry is crisp and golden, and the filling is firm (about 30 to 35 minutes).[9]

Low-growing strawberries provide an attractive edging to the boardwalk path through the kitchen garden and are convenient for picking when the fruit is ripe. Before strawberry plants set fruit, the leaves may be used to make tea.
GERALD H. EMMERICH JR.

Strawberry or Raspberry Cold Soup
(Erdbeeren-oder Himbeeren-Kaltschale)

No cooking is required for this refreshing, fresh-from-the-garden, cold soup. Historically popular throughout Germany, this recipe arrived in America with the immigrants in the mid-nineteenth century. Raspberries may be substituted for the strawberries. For 2 cups of fruit, add 2 to 3 cups of the wine and water mixture.

Remove the stems from the strawberries, wash them, put them in a bowl and sprinkle them with plenty of sugar. After half an hour, pour a mixture of half white wine, half water (mixed with ⅓ pound of sugar to a bottle of wine) and some cinnamon over the berries, and set to cool, if possible, on ice.[10]

Cold Red Pudding *(Kalter rother Pudding)*

This is a delicious and relaxing end to a fine meal. Don't consume too large a portion unless you bring a designated driver. Cornstarch may be substituted for potato starch.

Stir a quart of red wine, a pint of red currant juice, a pint of water, a half pound of sugar, and three ounces of fine potato starch together over a hot fire until it begins to boil, and then immediately pour into a mold that is floating in cold water.[11]

NORWEGIAN SETTLER GARDENS

5

From Subsistence to Economic Independence

The story of early Norwegian settlers who traveled to the American frontier is one of struggle, perseverance, and unrelenting toil. They left their beloved homeland plagued by its overpopulation, inadequate farm acreage, and economic hardships, with hope for a better life, greater opportunities, and a prosperous future for their children.

The earliest Norwegian pioneers arrived in America in 1825. Mass migration began in the 1830s, and by 1860 nearly seventy thousand people had emigrated from Norway to America.[1] These immigrants endured physical and emotional hardships on the long journey to the new country. Many arrived with little or no money, inadequate tools, and few supplies to face the challenges ahead, and yet they persevered.

Groups of Norwegian immigrants established their first Wisconsin settlements in the south-central and southeastern areas of the state in the late 1830s and 1840s. These early colonies became destinations for future immigrants, who then moved on to establish new settlements throughout the Midwest.

Industrious, frugal, and accustomed to hard work, Norwegian immigrants quickly fashioned crude shelters for housing and began breaking sod and clearing land for planting. Although they settled near others from their homeland and maintained ties with their Lutheran church, these farmers led fairly isolated lives in nineteenth-century Wisconsin. The all-important family unit provided the labor force and the focus of daily life.

The word *leisure* was not part of the vocabulary of Norwegian pioneers as they struggled to survive. A clear division of labor, firmly established in the Old Country, continued in the New World. Men hunted, trapped, and fished for food, and they cured animal hides. They cleared and cultivated the land, planted and harvested field crops, and eventually hauled those crops to market. They chopped wood, erected buildings, built fences, and fashioned furniture and utensils from wood.

Previous spread: Corn, pumpkins, carrots, turnips, and potatoes are visible in the family garden adjacent to the Knud and Gertrude Fossebrekke cabin at Old World Wisconsin.
GERALD H. EMMERICH JR.

Hungry early settlers found wild turkeys to be fair game.
TERRY MOLTER

Women handled the domestic scene—and beyond. They gave birth; raised large families; cared for the sick; cooked and baked; churned butter; made cheese, wine, and cider; brewed ale; and preserved food. They made candles and soap, did laundry, and cleaned house. They sheared sheep; carded, dyed, spun, and wove wool; and made and mended clothes for the family. Girls learned to knit at a young age and sometimes fastened balls of yarn to their skirts so they could knit while walking.[2] In addition:

> *It was of course the woman who should care for both the pigs and the cows. She should be the first up in the morning, make the fire, go out to the barn to feed the animals, milk the cows, and let the calves drink; then in to make breakfast and dress the children. The men weren't used to milking cows in the Old Country; because it was the woman who did all such, and then everybody thought it was only proper that she do it here too. She also had to take part in haying in the summertime. She should stack the hay, help with getting it in . . . and when evening came her program was: to milk, care for the calves and pigs, prepare supper for herself and family and then get the children to bed. Finally, when it was about eleven o'clock, she was finished with her day's work if the children did not screech or scream too much in the nighttime. But if she had a lot to do, she got paid for it. Usually she got one or two calico dresses a year, a pair of shoes that cost $1.75; and a hat that cost $1.50 every third year.*[3]

The Norwegian farmwife also raised poultry for eggs and meat for the family's use, and she often participated in slaughtering. Although little mention is made of the kitchen garden, the responsibility for that, too, fell on the woman's shoulders.

Children also helped with chores. They picked fruit, gathered nuts, hauled water and firewood, and helped care for the livestock. Boys helped in the farm fields, and girls assisted with household work. All hands were welcome. Norwegians took great pride in their large families, in which every member contributed valuable labor and no cash wages needed to be paid. It is not surprising that Norwegian girls—recognized as energetic and hardworking—found themselves in great demand as domestic servants in Yankee homes.

This prosperous Norwegian family had moved on to an elegant two-story home by the 1870s, when this photograph was taken. Here they share coffee outside their first residence, a primitive log house. Hollyhocks stand tall behind the table.
WHI IMAGE ID 27116

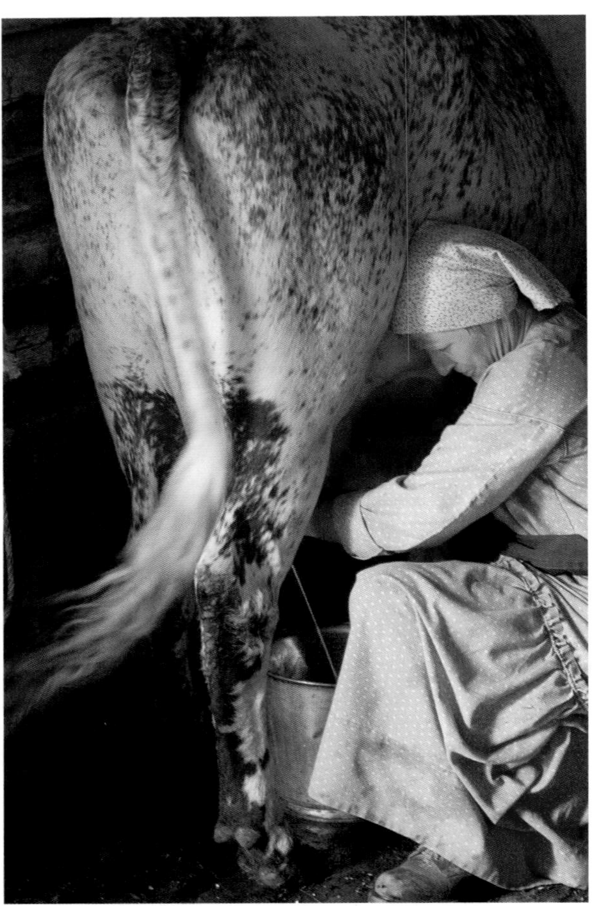

Opposite page, clockwise: Women's work: carding wool
SANDRA MATSON

Women's work: milking the family cow
LOYD HEATH

Pork became the meat most frequently served. The Ossabaw pictured here is one of several historic breeds of swine visitors may meet at Old World Wisconsin.
LOYD HEATH

More women's work: freshly dyed skeins of woolen yarn. Yellow onion skins, black walnuts, and red onion skins yield a variety of colorful shades in the dye bath.
SANDRA MATSON

Midwestern America offered great opportunities to own land and to make a new life, but Norwegian immigrants came unprepared for the frigid winters, sweltering summers, isolation, and homesickness they experienced. Even their diets required adjustment. Norwegians longed for the traditional foods from their homeland, made with rye, oats, barley, plentiful dairy products, dried saltwater fish, and assorted dried meats. In Wisconsin, wheat was the prevailing grain and pork became the meat most frequently served. Inexpensive and prolific, the pig required little maintenance and provided a fine source of protein. Served hot, cold, fresh, salted, pickled, pressed, or as bacon, pork often appeared at the table three times each day. When a family could afford to add one or more milk cows to the farmstead, the familiar dairy products produced brought great comfort. Coffee, frequently enjoyed in the Old Country, continued to be popular in Norwegian-American homes. At Christmastime special treats prepared to celebrate the holiday included pickled pig's feet, headcheese, and home-brewed beer.

The kitchen gardens of these immigrants offered little variety. Potatoes—familiar and sometimes brought from the homeland—were often the first crop planted and quickly became a staple in the diet of the Norwegian-Americans. Onions, rutabagas or Swede turnips, and possibly other turnip varieties complete the list of the earliest kitchen vegetables. Carrots, beets, and cabbage were soon added to the garden plots, and some families grew cucumbers, which gained popularity when pickled. Thyme, parsley, sweet marjoram, caraway, and dill provided a bit of flavoring to various dishes. By the 1860s Norwegian immigrants had been introduced to watermelons—native to Africa but grown in America since the seventeenth century—which they received enthusiastically and enjoyed fresh, cooked down for a molasses-type sweetener, and brewed for juice.[4] Norwegian immigrants adopted pumpkins and corn, previously unfamiliar New World crops, soon after livestock joined the farms. Both crops grew well and provided valuable nourishment for the animals yet apparently were never eaten by the families. But, ever frugal, the Norwegian-Americans found that when torn into narrow strips, cornhusks made fine material for stuffing mattresses.

Few Norwegians acquired any great fondness for green vegetables, even after they were readily available. In the early twentieth century, one aunt's traditional Norwegian recipes, lovingly prepared and shared half a century earlier, were fondly recalled: "Talk to me about modern cooking schools, salads and greens, pumpkin-pie, and Boston baked beans,—now that we are thoroughly Americanized, we manage to live on 'grass and such things,' but when it comes to the 'really and truly' goodies, give me Aunty Weglie's lefse and 'fattingmansbakkels,' Prim and Ost, etc. Talking about 'Ost,' why her 'Gammelost' had a flavor and aroma that put the modern Limburger out of commission."[5]

Opposite page, clockwise: A great asset to any pioneer farmer, oxen pulled tree stumps, broke sod, and plowed soil.
GERALD H. EMMERICH JR.

Norwegians historically excelled at growing tobacco in Wisconsin and have continued to do so for more than 150 years.
GERALD H. EMMERICH JR.

Sheep frequently joined Wisconsin farms, providing valuable wool.
NANCY L. KLEMP

Fruit brightened the cuisine. Wild fruits including raspberries, blackberries, plums, grapes, and cherries became ingredients for juices, jams, jellies, fruit soups, and homemade wines. Eventually rhubarb, currants, gooseberries, and strawberries joined the garden.

Letters and diaries written by early Norwegian immigrants offer little information about their rural kitchen gardens. Apparently vegetables (or the lack of them) did not inspire people to write. Given their never-ending workload and the limited variety the gardens produced, it is not surprising that when Norwegian-Americans wrote of plants, they penned words of flowers, potted plants, and delights of nature—all sources of pleasure and escape from the daily toil.

Norwegian women loved their flowers. They admired the wildflowers that grew abundantly and sent children to gather them. Some dug flowers from the woods and prairies to transplant them on their own property. As early as the 1850s Norwegian-American women wrote of roses and lilies and enjoyed the lovely fragrance of mignonette.[6] Letters requesting seeds and plants from the homeland crossed the ocean. Norwegian settlers exchanged plants with one another. Potted plants brought cheer to work-filled lives, and miracles of nature elicited great joy, as seen in this passage from a mid-nineteenth-century Norwegian immigrant's diary:

> *My kitchen table consists of a box we brought from Norway. . . . This we inverted and provided with four legs, beautifully trimmed and polished by nature herself, from a poplar tree growing in the woods just outside our door. To be sure they were frozen and raw, but what of it? . . . To my great delight, I discover that the legs have been sprouting lovely green side branches, covered with green leaves. Behold, thus our kind God causes summer to flourish in our home while winter still prevails outside.*[7]

Although visitors commented on the overcrowded, untidy, and none-too-clean rural homes, the Norwegian people were renowned for their generous hospitality. Guests commonly received a warm welcome, a meal, and even lodging when needed.

The Lutheran Church exerted considerable influence over the social and spiritual aspects of the lives of these immigrants and bound them together in close-knit communities. Education was highly valued, and all children attended school. Norwegian-American newspapers, written in Norwegian, brought news and information about both the homeland and the new country. These papers offered readers the opportunity to exchange ideas and share common interests while reinforcing their cultural identity.

A Norwegian family gathered for the photographer in front of their home, circa 1875. Potted plants enjoyed the sunny window, a cut-flower bouquet graced the table, and a vining plant decorated the doorway.
WHI IMAGE ID 26800

Framed by garden beds, a picket fence, and their American-style frame house, the family of Norwegian-born Anders Molstad posed for the camera, circa 1876.
WHI IMAGE ID 26681

Early Norwegian-American farmers struggled to provide food and shelter for their family's survival. They did most work by hand; the lucky ones were assisted by a team of oxen. Success for the future required the development of a working and profitable farm. These farmers grew wheat but soon recognized the need to diversify to reduce risk. In addition to broadening their crop base, many increased their livestock holdings and grew their own animal feed. They found particular success with dairy cows, sheep for wool, and tobacco.

Eventually larger, more comfortable homes replaced the quickly constructed rustic residences. Men adopted increased mechanization on the farms, which eased their workload. Long-standing gender roles shifted as men took over care of the livestock. Increasing wealth allowed leisure activities to seep into the lifestyle of Norwegian-American immigrants. Women directed their focus to home and family, leaving men to do the outside work. Despite the appearance of such American influences, Norwegians maintained close-knit communities and took great pride in their Norwegian identity. Ties with the Lutheran Church continued to be strong, and by the end of the century local and national societies celebrating Norwegian heritage began to organize and expand in America.

Determined to farm land of his own, Knud Crispinusen Fossebrekke joined others from his district in southeastern Norway and traveled to Wisconsin in 1839. Employed by a Yankee farmer near Rockford, Illinois, for two summers, Fossebrekke gained valuable knowledge and experience in American farming techniques and learned to speak and write English. He wintered in a dugout—a crude shelter excavated into the hillside—and used his earnings to purchase forty acres in the Town of Newark, Rock County, in 1841. A rough, one-room, one-and-a-half-story log house, sixteen and one-half feet by seventeen feet, provided shelter his second winter. Apparently a Norwegian couple who could not yet afford a farm of their own built the house for Fossebrekke while he worked near Rockford. In exchange for their labor they were allowed to live in the house temporarily. Exhibiting true Norwegian hospitality, Fossebrekke's small cabin sheltered as many as seventeen people during the first winters after it was built.[8]

In 1844 Fossebrekke married Gertrude Viker, recently arrived from a village near his birthplace. By 1845 they had cleared a few acres around the house and built a split-rail zigzag fence surrounding the property.[9] Potatoes, onions, and perhaps carrots and rutabagas or turnips likely were planted for their use. Wild game or pork supplemented their diet. Hand-planted pumpkins, corn, and wheat probably completed the crops; unfortunately, little documented evidence exists of early subsistence farmers' plantings.

Severe winter weather challenged the early settlers and their crudely built dwellings. Some wrote of bringing livestock inside the home to keep the animals from freezing. Others wrote of waking in the morning to find their bedding frozen. Nels Crispensen, one of the three Fossebrekke children, recalled early years in the family home almost a century later: "I can well remember when as kids we slept in an old home-made bed under a fur robe and in the winter mornings we often awoke under a pile of snow that had drifted through the chinks between the logs where the crude mortar had fallen out during the night."[10]

The Fossebrekkes' story is one of austere living conditions, never-ending toil and frugality, severe weather, and limited diet. But as the authors of a 1978 Old World Wisconsin unpublished manuscript noted, it is also a story of "hope, faith, and love, of optimism in the face of seemingly insurmountable odds in pushing back the forest to create a home in the wilderness."[11]

The Knud and Gertrude Fossebrekke log home, relocated from Rock County to Old World Wisconsin and restored to its 1845 appearance, provides a fine example of a Norwegian settler's first permanent cabin in Wisconsin. The re-created family garden, consisting of plots of potatoes, onions, carrots, rutabagas, and turnips, illustrates the lack of vegetable variety in the early Norwegian-American diet. A patch of thyme is grown for seasoning, and mint is enjoyed for tea. Wildflowers, including much-loved violets dug from the countryside, add a cheerful touch when transplanted to the home grounds. Corn and pumpkins are raised for animal feed, and a split-rail zigzag fence surrounds the home and adjacent cleared land, including the garden. The utilitarian nature of the farm and garden represents the basic subsistence level of the life of an early Wisconsin pioneer and his family.

Some immigrants came to the American Midwest under less-trying circumstances. Anders Ellingsen Kvaale, a landowner who sold his farm in Norway, traveled to Wisconsin in 1848 with his wife, Christina, and eight children. Financially comfortable, he arranged for a traditional Norwegian-style home to be built on their newly acquired 160-acre farm in the Town of Dunkirk, Dane County. The one-and-a-half-story home, finely crafted with tight-fitting logs, measured twenty-eight feet by twenty-two feet.[12]

HERBS FOR NORWEGIAN MEDICINAL USE

The use of plants for medicine in Norway dates back to the era of the Vikings, approximately 800–1000. Angelica, elderberry, gentian, juniper, onion, and plantain were considered especially useful.[1] Christianity arrived there around 1000; Cistercian monks, who had pioneered the tradition of the monastic garden—an enclosed area containing plants considered essential to daily life in a monastery, laid out in geometric beds divided by straight paths intersecting at right angles—introduced additional herbs as well as fruit trees.[2] Herbs continued to be grown for medicinal use throughout the nineteenth century. Valued plants included angelica, German chamomile, dock, elderberry flowers, hops, juniper, lavender, mugwort, onion, peppermint, Saint John's Wort, tobacco, turpentine (produced by distilling pine sap), valerian, wormwood, and yarrow. Both hops and valerian produced sedative effects. According to folk healers, angelica benefited people suffering from diverse ailments, including consumption, rheumatism, scurvy, food poisoning, dog bite, and the Black Death. It also was said to shield the wearer from evil incantations. Little wonder landowners were encouraged to plant angelica in 1164, and anyone caught stealing it incurred stiff punishment![3]

Bundles of herbs hung to dry.
SANDRA MATSON

When treating ailments, people tried home remedies first and often discussed treatments with neighbors, relatives, and friends. Sometimes they referred to "doctor books" for advice. If the illness persisted, they often consulted self-trained folk healers. Occasionally they saw professional doctors, but due to a shortage of Norwegian doctors in America, immigrants more frequently sought medical care from "wise women," superstitious old men, and unscrupulous quacks.[4]

NOTES

1. Kathleen Stokker, *Remedies and Rituals: Folk Medicine in Norway and the New Land* (St. Paul: Minnesota Historical Society Press, 2007), 6.

2. Karl-Dietrich Bühler, *The Scandinavian Garden* (London: Frances Lincoln Limited, 2000), 6.

3. Stokker, *Remedies and Rituals*, 108.

4. Ibid., 11.

The Anders and Christina Kvaale home, restored to its 1865 appearance at Old World Wisconsin. Morning glories climb up strings, washed and dyed wool hangs to dry, and potted geraniums brighten the porch.
NANCY L. KLEMP

Opposite page:
A Norwegian-American kitchen garden re-created at the Kvaale Farm
GERALD H. EMMERICH JR.

Kvaale recognized the advantage of diversification and raised a variety of crops and livestock. By 1860 his farm included two hundred acres, with sixty planted to crops. Wheat and barley brought in cash from sales of grain, and oats, hay, and corn were grown to feed livestock. Farm animals included hogs, cattle, sheep, and horses. Kvaale's sheep especially brought him considerable success, as wool commanded a fine price during and after the Civil War, due in part to a shortage of cotton from the Southern states.[13]

The Anders and Christina Kvaale family home, dismantled from its original location and rebuilt at Old World Wisconsin to its 1865 appearance, is central to a second Norwegian-American farmstead at the site. The re-created kitchen garden, easily accessible directly behind the house, provides onions, carrots, cabbage, beets, rutabagas, turnips, and cucumbers. Potatoes remained a staple in the Norwegians' diet even after they crossed the Atlantic and are well represented. Rhubarb, currants, gooseberries, strawberries, and watermelon join the vegetables as they often did in the 1860s. Caraway, chives, dill, marjoram, mint, parsley, and thyme provide tasty seasonings and flavorings for tea. While Norwegians favored split-rail fences, erected in a zigzag pattern, to surround fields and cropland, by 1860 horizontal board fences enclosed the yard and the garden with a more decorative appearance.[14]

Much-loved flowers and plants often grew near the house. Lilies and lilacs near the front door, morning glories climbing up strings to the porch roof, and old-fashioned hollyhocks brought color to lives of seemingly endless toil. Treasured potted plants smiled from windowsills or enjoyed summer out-of-doors. Geraniums, chrysanthemums, mignonette, myrtle, primroses, and even callas and fuchsias received special mention in the diaries of Norwegian ladies.[15]

Whether living in a dugout or crude cabin and struggling for survival, or enjoying a prosperous lifestyle in a comfortable, snugly built home, Norwegian-American women, sustained by their faith, looked to miracles of nature for respite from their work-filled days, finding moments of joy in the beauty of flowers.

Norwegian Recipes

Previous page:
Snug living quarters in the Knud and Gertrude Fossebrekke House at Old World Wisconsin make outdoor cooking facilities welcome.
GERALD H. EMMERICH JR.

Opposite page:
From left to right: flatbread, fresh eggs, and potato bread
SANDRA MATSON

Coffee

Nineteenth-century Norwegians favored coffee above all other beverages. At mealtime, during breaks from work, and whenever company visited, coffee played a key role in Norwegian hospitality.

½ cup ground coffee
1 egg, including shell

Mix coffee, egg, and shell together with enough water to moisten all of the grounds. Add to 1 quart of boiling water and cook 2 to 3 minutes. Set aside 10 minutes to settle. Either drain from grounds or pour slowly to avoid getting grounds in cup. Serve with cream and sugar, if available.[1]

Mint Tea

Norwegian pioneers gathered wild mint[2] and steeped a refreshing tea. The fresh or dried leaves of any flavorful mint may be used.

mint leaves, dried
sugar (small amount, if available)

Bring fresh cold water to boil. Place one large tablespoon of mint leaves per cup of tea to be made in pot and add boiling water. Let steep 5 minutes and serve with sugar (if available).[3]

Flatbread *(Flatbrød)*

Crispy *flatbrød*, often cited as Norway's national dish, may be made with the traditional mix of oats, rye, and barley or with whole wheat flour.

2 cups boiling water
2 cups yellow cornmeal
¼ cup butter
1 teaspoon salt
1 cup whole wheat flour

Pour boiling water on cornmeal, add butter, and beat well. Let the mixture get cold, then add other ingredients, adding enough flour to make a firm dough that can be easily handled. Roll very thin and bake slowly on ungreased griddle/stove-top.[4]

Opposite page: One step closer to headcheese, as the head is removed from the steaming kettle.
GERALD H. EMMERICH JR.

Lefse

***Lefse*, unleavened bread made with potatoes and traditionally served with home-churned butter, may be prepared on a griddle or frying pan.**

12 medium potatoes (to make 8 cups mashed)
8 heaping tablespoons butter
½ cup whipping cream, not whipped
1 teaspoon salt
4 cups flour

Peel potatoes, cook, and then mash with butter, cream, and salt. Let them get cold. Mix in flour and roll out rounds of dough paper thin on lightly floured board. Bake rounds on grill, turning until lightly brown on both sides.[5]

Headcheese

Headcheese was a special holiday treat, especially popular at Christmas. After the meat is drained and mixed with the herbs and spices, place it in a crock, and weigh the mixture down with a plate or lid (and a rock on the plate, if necessary) to pack it into a "cheese." After it has "set," slice and serve cold.

1 pig's head
⅜ teaspoon marjoram
⅜ teaspoon black pepper
1 teaspoon salt
⅜ teaspoon thyme

Remove eyes, brains, and nose from pig's head. Cut head in half or quarters and place in a large kettle. Cover with water and simmer over medium to medium-low heat for several hours or until meat is cooked. Remove meat from bones and place in a colander. Set colander in a baking pan and place in a warm oven to allow as much fat as possible to drip out. Mix drained meat with the spices. Place in a loaf pan and put in a cool location to set.[6]

Fish Soup *(Fiske Suppe)*

Norwegians have always been very fond of fish. When the beloved lutefisk was unavailable, at least they could enjoy fish soup.

2 pounds dressed fish with heads
2 carrots
1 small onion, chopped
2 medium potatoes, cubed
2 eggs
1 cup thick sour cream
2½ teaspoons salt
minced chives

Use a heavy, large saucepan with a tight-fitting cover. Rinse fish and drain well. With a sharp, heavy knife, cut the fish cross-wise into 1-inch slices. Put fish slices and heads into pot with 1 quart water and cook until tender. Meanwhile, cook the vegetables in a saucepan about 8 minutes or until tender. Remove the cooked fish and discard heads. Keep fish hot. Set aside 3 cups of fish broth, strained. Beat eggs until thick. Stir in cream and salt. Add fish liquid gradually, stirring constantly. Add vegetables and cook over low heat till heated through. Garnish soup with chives and serve. Fish is drained and served with boiled potatoes.[7]

Norwegian Stew *(Lapskaus)*

Potatoes and a variety of meats are easily combined to make a simple and filling traditional Norwegian one-pot meal.

1 soup plate of fresh meat
½ pound pork
1 quart potatoes
1 small onion
½ teaspoon pepper
salt
1 soup plate of boiled salt meat

Cut the fresh meat, pork, and potatoes into small cubes. Place over the fire in water. Add finely chopped onion, pepper, and salt to taste. Boil under cover for about 1½ hours. Add the salt meat after the fresh meat has boiled half an hour.[8]

Potato Flour

Potato flour is used to thicken gravy, soups, and stews and often appears in old European recipes.

Peel and grate potatoes. Spread the grated potatoes on a clean cloth and dry them in the sun. When they can be crumbled between your hands, they are done. Crumble and store in a sack in a dry place.[9]

Norwegian Cabbage with Sour Cream

A nice change from the ubiquitous potato, this recipe combines cabbage with one of the dairy products so often enjoyed by Norwegians.

1 medium cabbage, shredded
1½ teaspoons salt
½ teaspoon pepper
⅔ cup sour cream
1 tablespoon dill seed

Cook cabbage in just enough water to keep it from burning. Stir frequently. The cabbage should be tender, but still crisp. Stir in salt, pepper, sour cream, and dill seed. Cook covered over lowest possible flame 5 to 10 minutes, stirring frequently to prevent scorching. If necessary, add a little more sour cream.[10]

Introduced in America in the 1840s, Early Jersey Wakefield cabbage brings a delicious mild and sweet cabbage flavor to the table.
SANDRA MATSON

A medley of beets
NANCY L. KLEMP

Beet Salad *(Rodbette Salat)*

This dish provided a welcome change of color and flavors to excite mealtime!

2 or 3 boiled, chopped beets
1 large apple
¼ medium onion
5 whole allspice or small pinch ground allspice
½ cup vinegar
1 tablespoon sugar

Drain beets. Chop apple and onion, combine with beets. Add allspice, vinegar, and sugar. Let ripen overnight.[11]

Norwegian Rhubarb Custard (Grunnlav's Dessert)

Norway's Independence Day may be enjoyed with this springtime dessert, a traditional May 17 treat.

RHUBARB SAUCE:

1½ pounds rhubarb
½ cup water
1 cup sugar
1 tablespoon cornstarch
cold water

CUSTARD:

2 eggs
2 tablespoons sugar
1 cup milk
1 teaspoon vanilla
dash of allspice

Cut rhubarb into 2-inch pieces. Bring water and sugar to boil. Add rhubarb and simmer until almost tender. Remove rhubarb to serving bowl, leaving liquid in saucepan. Mix cornstarch in small amount of cold water. Remove saucepan from heat and stir in cornstarch. Return to heat. Simmer 3 minutes. Pour over rhubarb in serving bowl. Mix carefully. For the custard: Beat eggs and sugar until fluffy. Bring milk to boiling and add to egg mixture, beating vigorously. Put in saucepan and simmer until thick, beating constantly. Remove from heat; add vanilla and cool, stirring occasionally. Pour custard over rhubarb. Sprinkle with allspice.[12]

IRISH SETTLER GARDENS

6

From Shanty to Lace Curtains

Many immigrants arriving in America received a less-than-welcoming reception, but few faced widespread discrimination to the extent the Irish did. Yankees resented them in part due to the long history of mutual hostility between the Irish and the English. In addition, the majority of the Irish proudly and openly supported the Roman Catholic Church, which invited further criticism. Some described them as brutish, quarrelsome, unkempt, and even dirty, and they carried a reputation for drinking too much whiskey. Yet their gifts for storytelling and music brought admiration.

The Irish came to America seeking employment, a place to live, and enough food to sustain themselves. They arrived with limited skills, most having labored on small farms in their homeland. Willing to work hard, they readily accepted employment that required arduous manual labor, including jobs in mines, in the logging industry, and in construction, working on roads, railroads, and canals.

Some Irishmen toiled in Wisconsin's lead mines as early as the 1820s and 1830s. But with the onslaught of the Great Potato Famine in Ireland after the mid-1840s, their fellow countrymen began arriving in massive numbers. A destructive fungal disease swept through the Emerald Isle's potato crops, wreaking havoc on the country's main food source. This devastation, combined with years of social and political oppression and continuing economic struggles, led to massive emigration. Between 1845 and 1854, approximately 1.5 million people left Ireland, and the vast majority journeyed to America.[1]

By midcentury, twenty-one thousand people of Irish birth lived in Wisconsin; by 1860 that number had more than doubled to fifty thousand.[2] Most gravitated to cities, preferably near a Catholic church, close to other family members, and where job opportunities existed. Some went on to purchase and farm their own land, which had been just a dream in the Old Country. They brought optimism that with good

Previous spread:
A charming cottage garden in the front yard of the restored Mary Hafford House overflows with plants familiar from the Emerald Isle.
TERRY MOLTER

A woman willing to wash laundry for others during the nineteenth century could earn extra income to support her family.
NANCY L. KLEMP

old-fashioned hard work and a bit of Irish luck a better life could be obtained and they could exert at least some control over their lives.

The story of the Irish is also one of strong women and their determination to sustain and help improve the lives of their family members. More women came to America from Ireland than from any other European nation. Many arrived unmarried and in search of work. Just as the men did, the Irish women experienced discrimination and accepted jobs others might avoid. Many became domestic servants, while others took positions in factories and textile mills or worked on farms. Money earned and sent back to the homeland frequently paved the way for other family members to come to America.

Married women also found ways to earn extra income and contribute to the family's finances. On the farm they sold poultry and dairy products. Women with children invariably chose to work at home and took in mending, laundry, and piecework or even housed boarders. These assertive and resourceful women viewed themselves as fairly self-sufficient, which proved especially beneficial to the unfortunate many who became widows due to the dangerous work their husbands pursued. Mother represented the center and the strength of the Irish immigrant family. The affection between parents and their children, and among siblings, strengthened through immigration. Kinship was key to Irish existence.

Little documentation exists about gardens of the nineteenth-century Irish in Wisconsin. Gardens of their homeland and those of densely Irish settlements in the eastern United States offer some insight into traditional gardening styles and favorite plants.

In Ireland the stately country homes of the wealthy showcased extensive gardens, often enclosed and protected by stone walls. These gardens of the elite, with their formal paths, decorative flower and shrub borders, and espaliered fruit trees,[3] hardly bore a resemblance to the rural countryside peasant farms and gardens.

Eighty percent of all farms in Ireland measured fewer than fifteen acres during the first half of the nineteenth century.[4] A tenant farmer planted three-quarters of his land to be harvested for the landlord in exchange for the opportunity to use the remaining quarter for his own family's needs. The vast majority of that land was planted to potatoes, which were inexpensive and easy to grow and store, generally producing large quantities of nutritious food for people and livestock.[5] When the crop did well, it was not unusual for a working man to eat fourteen pounds of potatoes at a meal.[6] An average consumption of eight pounds of that popular vegetable per day *for each family member* was well documented.[7] A small family of two parents and three children could easily consume a bushel of potatoes each day, and the Irish valued *large* families: the entire family contributed labor to the farm, so more hands meant more help. Also, Irish superstition equated large families with success in the crops and livestock.[8]

Once the previous year's harvest had been depleted, meal options looked lean. Milk, occasionally fish, and even more rarely meat supplemented the nineteenth-century Irish diet that relied so heavily on the potato. It seems that the Irish never grew a wide variety of vegetables. E. Estyn Evans noted in *Irish Folk Ways* that by the time the plow replaced cultivation by hand and spade "a vegetable garden [was] a rare thing, at best a tiny plot left to the care of the woman."[9] Cabbage, leeks, onions, turnips or rutabagas, cresses, and edible seaweed, as well as oats and wheat for bread received occasional mention in his extensive study, but the preponderance of the potato in the diet cannot be overemphasized.

In the eastern United States, more than two thousand Irish immigrants settled in northern Delaware in the nineteenth century to work in the E. I. du Pont de Nemours and Company's black powder industry. Families there maintained "very small" kitchen gardens, averaging thirty to forty feet wide by forty to sixty feet long. Rectangular beds

DINNER—AND SO MUCH MORE!

Sir Walter Raleigh receives credit for introducing both potatoes and cabbage to Ireland in the 1580s.[1] At that time suspected to be poisonous to people, both vegetables originally found use as animal feed. More than one hundred years later they were deemed safe for human consumption but were considered fit only as food for peasants. Potatoes, of course, became the primary food of Ireland.

Even before it met the dinner kettle, cabbage had been lauded for its healing properties. Medieval textbooks recommended a poultice of thoroughly macerated fresh green cabbage leaves to treat burns, gout, sore legs, ulcers, and wounds.[2] By the end of the eighteenth century the Irish appreciated cabbage for its value as high-yielding animal fodder as well as its versatility at the family dinner table.

Rutabagas and turnips, inexpensive and easily grown, were also adapted to uses beyond the kitchen. With the top cut off and the bottom trimmed to sit flat, a hole was carved into the top of the vegetable so a candle could be seated into the opening. Traditionally these homemade candleholders were lit

Large, firm heads of cabbage—such as this Late Flat Dutch variety—store well, ensuring a long season of usage. NANCY L. KLEMP

DINNER—AND SO MUCH MORE!

THE PUMPKIN EFFIGY.

The jack-o'-lantern blended the Irish tradition of hollowing and carving a turnip or rutabaga with the New World pumpkin to create an American symbol of Halloween. This image appeared in the September 1875 issue of *The Ladies' Floral Cabinet and Pictorial Home Companion*.

and placed in the front windows of the house at Christmastime to provide an especially warm glow.[3] At Halloween, these same vegetables were hollowed out and carved to resemble faces. Placed inside and lit, candles accentuated the carvings. This Irish tradition continued in America and grew in popularity when the New World pumpkin became the vegetable of choice to be carved into jack-o'-lanterns.

NOTES

1. Margaret M. Mulrooney, *Black Powder, White Lace: The du Pont Irish and Cultural Identity in Nineteenth-Century America* (Hanover, NH, and London: University Press of New England, 2002), 175.
2. Patrick Logan, *Irish Country Cures* (New York: Sterling Publishing Co. Inc., 1994), 105, 110.
3. *Christmas in Ireland* (Chicago: World Book Inc., 1985), 65.

The monotonous diet of the Irish country folk revolved around potatoes—rows and rows of potatoes.
GERALD H. EMMERICH JR.

Irish Cobbler potatoes
NANCY L. KLEMP

predominated, with a straight central path through the garden and two-foot paths around the edges. Men turned and fertilized the garden plots; women and children planted and maintained them. As in their homeland, the entire family worked together at harvest time. Inexpensive and easily grown and stored vegetables dominated the gardens. Several rows—and sometimes as much as half the garden—of potatoes ensured a supply of the familiar staple. Cabbage, too, earned space in the garden. Other vegetables grew in lesser quantities, as the Irish immigrants eagerly adopted new foods, preferably those that could be boiled for mealtime.[10] In the Emerald Isle, built-in ovens had been rare. The long-standing Irish tradition of boiling vegetables, soups, stews, and porridges continued to be the most popular method of food preparation in their newly adopted country.

A typical nineteenth-century Irish-American home in Wisconsin would likely have included a small vegetable garden—rectangular with a straight path cut through the center—in the backyard, out of view to the casual visitor. Potatoes would have dominated the space, accompanied by smaller beds of cabbage, leeks, onions, rutabagas, turnips, and parsley. The Irish immigrants were observant and quick to adopt new plants they met, but they did not abandon those associated with their ethnic heritage.

The Irish viewed America as a true land of opportunity, a country in which they could gain respectability and rise in society. Putting the image of dirty, disorderly, uncomfortable shanty homes behind them, men became successful breadwinners, and women sought to create genteel home environments. Decorative objects and furnishings appropriate for a parlor dressed up the front room of the house. That front room might combine the functions of the kitchen and dining room as well as the parlor, and the decorative pieces might be homemade or secondhand rather than newly store-bought finery, but they were indicative of the Irish intention to acculturate into American society. Attractive plant stands showcased charming potted plants. Linen tablecloths and white lace curtains, in particular, symbolized the refinement and respectability they sought. By displaying Irish linen and Irish lace, the quickly adapting immigrants identified pride and loyalty to their Irish heritage as well as to America.

Mary Ward Hafford, her husband, Matthew, and their young son immigrated to America from Ireland in 1864. By the time they settled in the Village of Hubbleton, Jefferson County, in 1867, they had two additional children. Matthew passed away suddenly in 1868, and Mary found herself needing to earn support for her family.[11] Exhibiting

When the Mary Hafford home was relocated from the Village of Hubbleton to Old World Wisconsin, it was rebuilt atop a hill overlooking a restored prairie.
LOYD HEATH

the strength and spirit of strong Irish women before her, she became a washerwoman, which enabled her to care for her children at home while doing laundry for others. Through hard work she prospered, and although she never learned to read or write English,[12] Mary lived the dream of seeing her children receive a formal education and become respected members of the community. She purchased property and in 1885 moved into her own newly built home.[13] Modest but comfortable, this home in America represented Mary Hafford's climb up the social ladder and her rise in respectability, and it gave her a place to proudly hang her lovely Irish lace curtains.

THE ROSE: THE QUEEN OF ALL FLOWERS

For centuries roses truly have been considered the queen of all flowers. In 1825 Elizabeth Kent penned words of enthusiasm for the beloved rose:

> *Poetry is lavish of Roses; it heaps them into beds, weaves them into crowns, twines them into arbors, forges them into chains, adorns with them the goblet used in the festivals of Bacchus, plants them in the bosom of beauty,—Nay, not only delights to bring in the Rose itself upon every occasion, but seizes each particular beauty it possesses as an object of comparison with the loveliest works of nature:—as soft as a Rose leaf; as sweet as a Rose; Rosy-clouds; Rosy-cheeks; Rosy-lips; Rosy-blushes; Rosy-dawns, etc., etc.*[1]

NOTE

1. Elizabeth Kent, *Flora Domestica, or The Portable Flower-Garden* (London: Taylor and Hessey, 1825), 265.

Fragrant old-fashioned roses invite visitors to pause outside the restored home of Mary Hafford at Old World Wisconsin.
TERRY MOLTER

PLANTS BEYOND THE KITCHEN GARDEN

Although the early Irish immigrants rarely planted gardens exclusively of flowers, they brought memories and an appreciation of all living things from the beloved land left behind. Even Irish horticulturalist William Robinson (1838–1935) carried the inspiration of the woodlands and wildflowers as well as the simple gardens of the cottagers of his native country into his writings and garden designs for the elite of England and beyond.

Those remembering the Old Country might have chosen to plant some of the following plants, all fondly remembered from their Irish homeland: buttercup, wild carrot, white daisy, foxglove, heather, iris, Johnny-jump-up, lavender, lily, corn marigold, pot marigold, may flower, nasturtium, periwinkle, primrose, rose, wallflower. Yarrow might be cut on Midsummer's Eve and hung in the house to ward off illness.

Familiar herbs included lemon balm, chamomile, sweet cicely, hyssop, lovage, marjoram, parsley, southernwood, and tansy. Some were used for tea, others became ingredients in sachets or insect repellent blends, and some added their magic to potions and spells.

Elderberry, holly, rowan, and whitethorn also earned respect. Ferns grew so fern seed—said to render men invisible—might be collected for its magical powers![1]

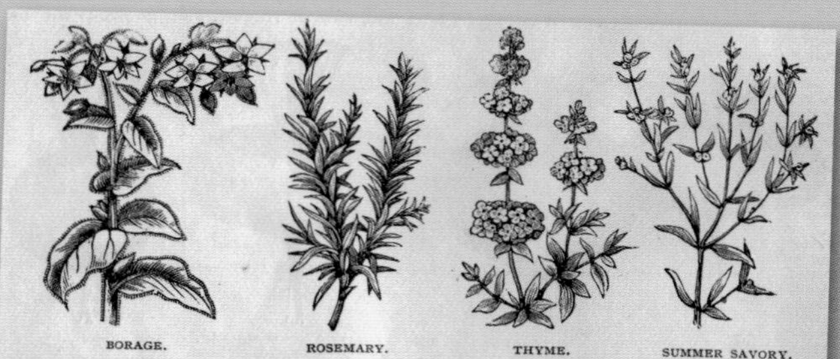

bunches and hung in the shade. For soups and dressing for poultry these herbs are a necessi in the estimation of most persons, while as domestic medicines several kinds are held in hi repute. The Sage and its uses, of course, every one is acquainted with. The Broad-leav English is the best. Thyme is of universal cultivation, as is also Summer Savory. Rosema is a very fragrant herb, and is everywhere popular. Borage is a beautiful plant, with azure bl flowers, pretty enough for any flower garden. It is much used in Europe for flavoring Cla and other wines. We give a list of the herbs generally cultivated and prized, either by the co or the nurse.

Anise,	Cumin,	Marjoram, Sweet,	Savory, Winter,
Balm,	Dill,	Rosemary,	Thyme, Broad-Leav English,
Basil, Sweet,	Fennel, Large Sweet,	Rue,	Thyme, Summer,
Borage,	Horehound,	Saffron,	Thyme, Winter,
Caraway,	Hyssop,	Sage,	Wormwood.
Coriander,	Lavender,	Savory, Summer,	

A very small space in the garden will give all the herbs needed in any family. The cult is very simple, and the best way is to make a little seed-bed in the early spring, and sow t

seeds, then set the plants out as soon as large enough in a bed or border. The trouble, the fore, is trifling, while the expense is comparatively nothing. Keep the soil about the plants cl and mellow, and they will make a rapid growth. In a mild climate some kinds will live over winter, but they are so easily raised from seed that saving old plants is not of much consequen

A listing of "sweet and pot" herb seeds available for purchase from Vick's Seed Company in 1876 *VICK'S FLOWER AND VEGETABLE GARDEN*

NOTE

1. E. Estyn Evans, *Irish Folk Ways* (New York: The Devin-Adair Company, 1957); Patrick Logan, *Irish Country Cures* (New York: Sterling Publishing Co. Inc., 1994); Terence Reeves-Smyth, *The Garden Lover's Guide to Ireland* (New York: Princeton Architectural Press, 2001); William Robinson, *The English Flower Garden* (New York: The Amaryllis Press, 1984).

Even when they were far from wealthy, Irish-American women enjoyed creating warm and welcoming home environments.
TERRY MOLTER

Fragrant lilacs, roses, and lavender welcome visitors to the Mary Hafford House, which was restored to its 1885 appearance after being moved to Old World Wisconsin from the Village of Hubbleton, Jefferson County, in 1980. Inspired by plants familiar from Hafford's homeland, a small cottage garden abounds with flowers and herbs. Located in the front yard near the main entrance to the house, the garden is situated to be admired. This small, well-tended jewel is lush with sweet pinks, violets, and wallflowers; delicate harebells and daisy-like chamomile; cowslips and calendulas in shades of sunshine gold; umbels of soft white yarrow; and spiky hyssop. Alpine strawberries luxuriate among the flowers, and gray santolina, placed intermittently along the borders, stands guard against inquisitive bunnies. Inside the house, a wire plant stand in the front room holds treasured potted plants such as ivy and flowering and rose-scented geraniums.

By 1885 Mary Hafford had been in America for more than twenty years. Comfortably settled in her community, she was mindful of current gardening and decorating trends. By planting a decorative garden in the front yard in the American style and filling it with plants of her homeland, she maintained her ties and loyalty to both countries.

Irish Recipes

Previous page:
Tea and Irish soda bread in the Mary Hafford House at Old World Wisconsin
LOYD HEATH

Irish Soda Bread

This classic hearty Irish bread is a wonderful accompaniment for soups, stews, and boiled dinners. Our recipe, from the Miller family of County Roscommon, dates to 1857. Baking soda serves as the leavening agent.

6 cups flour (or 4 cups whole wheat flour and 2 cups white flour)
1 teaspoon of bicarbonate of soda (baking soda)
1 teaspoon salt (if using buttermilk, add about 2 tablespoons)
1 cup buttermilk, sour milk, or fresh milk (if using fresh milk, add 1 teaspoon of cream of tartar to dry ingredients)

Mix dry ingredients together and make a well in the center. Add enough milk to make a thick dough. Stir with wooden spoon, mixing lightly. Add a little milk if using whole wheat and it seems too stiff. Put onto lightly floured board or table and flatten dough into circle about 1½ inches thick. Put on baking sheet or pie pan. Cut a large cross over it with floured knife to ensure even distribution of heat. Let stand for about 20 to 25 minutes before baking. Bake in moderate [350 to 375 degree] oven for about 40 minutes.[1]

Boiled Dinner

Boiled foods are traditional in Ireland. Any vegetables may be added and simmered until tender. Root vegetables are especially well suited for this one-pot meal.

In a large kettle or saucepan simmer pork hocks and pork pieces in several quarts of cold water. Season with salt and pepper. Prepare cabbage, carrots, potatoes, and onions by first slicing into hunks (and then mincing finely in a large chopping bowl with a chopping knife, if desired). Add to pork stock. Small potatoes and onions can be added whole. Serve from platter onto deep dishes or soup bowls.[2]

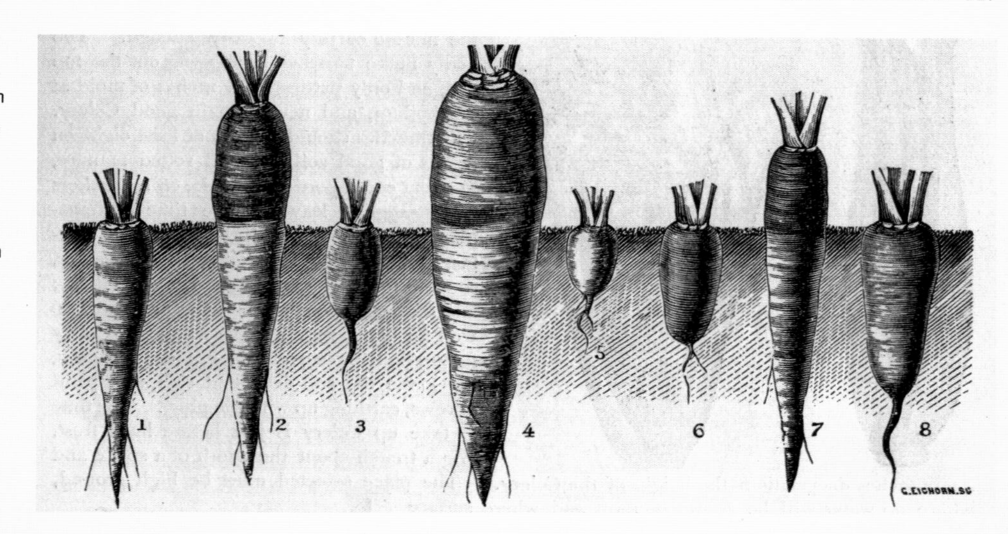

This engraving shows the comparative size and growth habit of the leading varieties of carrots in 1876: 1. Long Orange; 2. Orange Belgian Green-Top; 3. Early French Short-Horn; 4. White Belgian Green-Top; 5. Early Very Short Scarlet; 6. Half-Long Scarlet Stump-Rooted; 7. Altringham; 8. Half-Long Scarlet

VICK'S FLOWER AND VEGETABLE GARDEN

Creamed Cod Over Boiled Potatoes

Salt cod added flavor to the mountains of bland potatoes consumed by the Irish in the nineteenth century.

codfish, salted and dried (salt cod)
cold water
2 potatoes
1 small onion, chopped
salt
flour
butter
milk

Flake cod and place it in a pan of cold water; allow it to soak overnight. In the morning place the cod in fresh cold water in a covered saucepan. Heat the cod on the stove to scalding point; do not boil.

Wash potatoes and cut off ends; let them stand in cold water for a few hours. Put the potatoes and onion into a pan of boiling water, cover, and keep boiling constantly. After 15 minutes, throw in some salt and boil for another 15 minutes. Test with fork.[3]

After draining the cod, add flour, butter, and milk to make a cream sauce. Serve immediately over boiled potatoes.

Borreen Brack

***Borreen brack* translates to "speckled loaf"—a reference to the currants in the bread. Traditionally the loaves were measured by the size of a woman's fist: two fists long, two fists wide, and one fist thick. A "small spoon" is equal to a teaspoon.**

1 cup scalded milk
½ cup freshly churned butter, salted
3 large eggs
⅔ cup sugar
1 large spoon of barm (beer yeast)
5 cups flour
1 small spoon salt
1 small spoon allspice
1½ cups currants
melted butter
additional sugar

Pour scalded milk over butter to melt; cool. Mix well eggs, sugar, and barm and add to cooled milk mixture. Mix in flour, salt, allspice, and currants. Knead the dough thoroughly and then place in a buttered bowl and cover. Let rise to double in bulk. Turn out and punch down. Divide dough and put into 2 buttered pans. Cover and let rise again until doubled in bulk. Bake at 350 degrees for 30 to 45 minutes. By this time it should be browned and done. Brush the loaves with melted butter and sprinkle with sugar.[4]

Fresh Fruit Bottled

Bottling fresh fruit offered an alternative to drying as a method of preservation in a damp climate. Burning a match in the bottle displaced air and replaced it with a sulfurous acid gas that acts as a preservative.

fresh fruit of all kinds (let the fruit be full grown)

Have some perfectly dry glass bottles and some nice soft corks. Burn a match in each of the bottles and quickly place fruit in to be preserved. Gently cork the bottles. Put them into a very cool oven until the fruit has shrunk away a fourth. Beat the corks in tight, cut off the top, cover with wax. Keep in a dry place.[5]

Sponge Cake

A simple sponge cake, made from this recipe dating to 1876, provides a perfect sweet touch to the end of any meal. A "quick" or hot oven referred to how fast the oven was burning and was equivalent to 400 degrees.

3 eggs
1 cup sugar
1 cup flour
1½ teaspoons baking powder

Separate the eggs and beat yolks and sugar together. Mix in flour and baking powder. Beat egg whites until stiff but not dry; fold into mixture. Pour into a well-oiled loaf pan and bake in a quick oven.[6]

Potato Candy

This is another tribute to the Irish sweet tooth—and another recipe for potatoes!

1 cup warm, unseasoned mashed potatoes
½ teaspoon salt
2 teaspoons vanilla
about 2 pounds confectioners' sugar

Combine potatoes, salt, and vanilla in mixing bowl. Sift sugar over potatoes, about 1 cup at a time, stirring constantly, until mixture is like a stiff dough. Knead well, adding more sugar as needed. Cover with a damp cloth and chill until a small spoonful can be rolled into a ball. Shape into small balls. Makes about 2 pounds.[7]

Cough Syrup

This cough syrup recipe seems a bit intense, but it is surely preferable to an old Irish treatment for whooping cough that recommended boiling the droppings of sheep in milk and giving the mixture to the patient![8]

One pint of the best vinegar. Break into it an egg and leave in the shell and all, overnight (or longer). In the morning it will all be eaten except the white skin, which must be taken out. Then add one pound of loaf sugar and take a tablespoon three times a day, for an adult. This is a most excellent remedy for a cough in any stage.[9]

DANISH SETTLER GARDENS

7

The Value of Community and Cooperation

Some people have a penchant for seeing the bright side in life; the Danes are such a people. Despite the poverty and hardships they faced in the nineteenth century, they looked for ways to make a better life, valued every opportunity to learn, and maintained their open-minded, cheerful disposition and cooperative spirit.

Most Danes who came to Wisconsin in the 1840s and 1850s arrived in small groups and settled in various locations across the territory. Additional countrymen followed, and by 1870 Wisconsin was home to more than 5,200 Danish immigrants—a greater number than any other state.[1] While people from Norway and Sweden immigrated in larger numbers, the Danes contributed to the fabric of the region with their reasonable, contemplative approach to life, their value of relationships with others, and their sense of responsibility to community.

They arrived with a strong desire to control their own destiny and to become landowners. While some settled in cities (Racine became known as the most Danish city in America), many followed the dream of land ownership and built farms. One third-generation Danish-American recalled her grandfathers' farming experience in western Wisconsin in the late-nineteenth century:

> *Since Wisconsin was all forest in this area, so much hard work and patience was a must. Both of our Grandfathers have told us that they didn't mind the hard work, as this was a chance for them to have a farm of their own. In Denmark then, conditions were bad, and a young man over there did not have much hope for the future except to work for the rich landowners, who in return, paid them very poorly.*[2]

Previous spread:
The Kristen Pedersen family home, relocated to Old World Wisconsin and restored to its 1890 appearance. Potatoes await digging in the re-created kitchen garden, which is surrounded by a vertical board fence.
GERALD H. EMMERICH JR.

Opposite page:
The Danes enjoyed both red and green cabbage in the garden and on the table.
GERALD H. EMMERICH JR.

A significantly greater number of men than women emigrated from Denmark to America, and Danish women found themselves highly prized. Marriage-minded men often had to look to other immigrant groups, and they frequently chose German wives. The wife of a Dane would be a partner beyond companionship and motherhood. She was also expected to work as hard as he did—sometimes right alongside of him, sharing the same tasks. Although Danish men admired Yankee ingenuity and technical advances, they had no designs on their stay-in-the-house women.

For the most part, Danes assimilated into the American environment fairly quickly. A few Danish-established communities attempted to keep the customs and language of the Old Country alive, but their children readily adopted the new country ways.

The Danish immigrants valued education; kept small, clean, comfortable homes; and enjoyed music, good books, conversation, and gardens.

The people of Denmark carry a long tradition of love for gardens. Their earliest plantings were utilitarian in nature.[3] Eventually influences of Italian and French Renaissance and Baroque designs spread through Europe and into southern Scandinavia. Gardens in Denmark incorporated some of those design elements,[4] although they never became as ostentatious as those in France and Italy.[5] In Denmark handsome gardens occupied clearly defined areas, enclosed by tall hedges that provided protection from winds.[6] Pleasure gardens—separated from utilitarian gardens and symmetrically laid out and edged with boxwood or low, shrubby herbs—followed the trends popular in parts of Europe, but the fancy terraces, pools, and fountains that were incorporated into the upscale French and Italian residences were not the choice of the Danes, who favored a more rustic, more natural design.

Although the working poor did not grow elaborate decorative gardens for themselves, the Danish seemed to have an innate appreciation of all plants, flowers, and orderly design. In Wisconsin, vertical board fences replaced living hedges. Closely spaced boards protected plantings from animals as well as winds.

In rural nineteenth-century Wisconsin, plants for food took top priority, with Danish immigrants growing most of what they ate. Immediately upon arrival, they put potatoes into the ground, and often in great quantities. Optimistic farmwives looked forward to boiling the potatoes and adding butter and parsley, or to sugar-browning or caramelizing them after boiling. Other root vegetables, especially beets, carrots, and onions, soon joined the first crop and could eventually be stored for winter use. Red and green cabbage, planted in neatly arranged beds, added color to the garden and offered the promise of numerous culinary possibilities, from sweet-and-sour preparations and soup to an accompaniment for pork. Planted in large quantities, frilly green kale and

parsley offered more wonderful soup ingredients. Parsley might also stuff a chicken, add flavor to gravy, and provide a decorative garnish. Peas, too, would be enjoyed fresh or dried to be rehydrated for winter meals. Navy beans were a welcome addition to the soup pot, perhaps with mashed potatoes and chopped onion, celery, and parsley added. Celery and possibly parsnips, cucumbers, and chives might be included in the selection. Caraway—its signature flavor an essential ingredient in the coarse, dark Danish rye bread—and dill—a lovely addition to the thinly sliced, marinated sweet-and-sour cucumbers—brought tall, feathery touches to the garden. The Danes commonly planted half-acre or larger kitchen gardens.

Mangel beets grew with the field crops, alongside the New World corn and pumpkins the Danish immigrants quickly adopted, to be chopped up for animal feed. Pumpkin plants provided convenient vines to tie up corn shocks. Hay and oats were planted for the livestock. Wheat and any barley not saved for soup were sold as grain for cash. Rye, originally brought from the homeland, was raised for the family's use. Coarsely ground, sometimes in the household coffee grinder, rye was the key ingredient for the traditional Danish dark loaves of bread. All of the crops were sown, harvested, and processed entirely by hand. Any surplus from the farm and garden meant the potential for additional income or might be traded for services. For example, some doctors accepted payment for their medical care in vegetables and farm products.[7]

Coffee, sugar, rice (for rice pudding), yeast, and spices that could not be grown at home had to be purchased. The frugal Danes had their eyes on those "splendid sugar trees"—as they were described in an 1875 real estate promotional brochure[8]—when sugar maples were found growing in the area. The sap could be processed to make maple syrup and sugar.

With the addition of the dairy cow, generally one of the Danes' first purchases in the New World, all things seemed possible. Milk was considered vital to the diet, especially for growing children. Prior to refrigeration, milk—when the cow supplied it—was served at every meal. Given a good supply of milk, grains, vegetables, and fish from local rivers, the Danes could continue the familiar diet of their homeland.

And they thoroughly enjoyed available fruit. Strawberries, gooseberries, raspberries, and black currants became jams, jellies, and puddings. Apple trees provided ingredients for *aeblekage* (apple cake), applesauce, and stuffing for the Christmas goose. Some Danes also tried their hand at planting pear, plum, and cherry trees. Whether productive or simply decorative, any trees on the north and west sides of the house provided windbreak and shade, but they were rarely permitted to grow too near the dwelling, as potential forest fires always posed a serious threat.[9]

Charming asters
SANDRA MATSON

Flowers, too, brought great joy. Daylilies, wild plums, and violets dug from the wild and transplanted to the home grounds provided immediate color. Carefully nurtured seeds matured to flowers in profusion in front of the house, around doorways, in small stone-ringed beds in the yard, and in the kitchen garden. The use of rounded rocks and circular beds harked back to earlier times in Denmark, when village elders formed a circle in the forest in order to administer justice.[10] Employed in the garden, the circular form offered a welcome connection to the homeland.

Tall, colorful hollyhocks; vining morning glories and sweet peas; fragrant petunias; and cheerful marigolds, nasturtiums, and zinnias all stirred fond memories in Danish-Americans years later recalling their nineteenth-century Midwestern gardens.[11] Charming asters, balsam, pansies, and phlox, and happy calendulas and snapdragons[12] were also warmly remembered. Roses[13] grew, too, and lilacs[14] in front of the house shared their

THE WHEELBARROW

Every man who has a rod of ground to cultivate should possess this machine. In small gardens it is sufficient for the conveyance of all manures, soils, products, etc., and in larger places it is always needed for use, where a cart cannot go.

—*The Fruit Garden; A Treatise* (1851)[1]

High praise for the necessity and practicality of the wheelbarrow abounds in nineteenth-century gardening manuals. A very early and commonly recommended form was made of wood with removable sidewalls and an iron-tired wooden wheel. Called a box wheelbarrow, it was favored in the garden because of its versatility and overall lighter weight. As with other agricultural implements used extensively out-of-doors, wheelbarrows were routinely painted to protect the wood from weathering; later manufactured examples were sometimes ornamented with stenciled motifs and pinstriping. As the century drew to a close, metal components were introduced in the bracing framework and new forms with beds of seamless, stamped galvanized steel competed with the sale of wheelbarrows in the traditional box style.

Canal barrows—wheelbarrows having very sturdy fixed beds designed for side dumping—might also have been found in the nineteenth-century garden. They could be handcrafted on the farm from reused barrel staves and old plow handles but were more commonly factory made. Used most frequently wherever exceptionally heavy loads were moved, such as coal in the blacksmith's shop or cordwood on the farm, canal barrows were equally useful in moving large harvests from the garden.

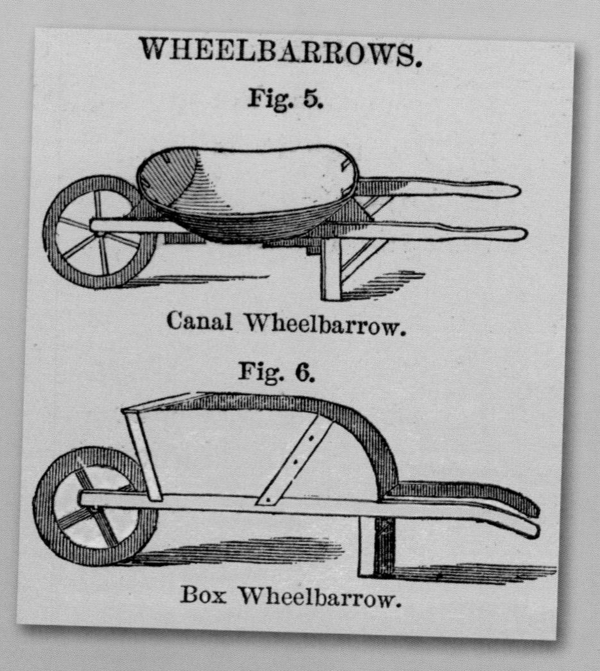

The canal and box wheelbarrows were the two most common wheelbarrow forms in use on the nineteenth-century farm in America.
ALEXANDER WATSON, *THE AMERICAN HOME GARDEN*

No matter its style, the wheelbarrow was an indispensable tool on the nineteenth-century Wisconsin farm. It remains equally essential to the contemporary gardener.

NOTE

1. P. Barry, *The Fruit Garden; A Treatise* (New York: Charles Scribner, 1851), 378.

THE WHEELBARROW

At Old World Wisconsin the new interprets the old. An exceptionally large box wheelbarrow in the historic site's collection was meticulously reproduced and put to use in the Sanford kitchen garden. Shown here laden with straw on its way to the garden, this wheelbarrow's sheer size deepens the visitor's appreciation for the amount of work involved in maintaining a large kitchen garden. The barrow's deep bed, measuring almost four feet in length, foreshadows the size of the expected harvest.
NANCY L. KLEMP

A modern, Amish-made garden or farm cart moves a heavy load of ripe pumpkins from the garden. This hand-pulled vehicle closely resembles an original farm cart in Old World Wisconsin's collection. The historic site's example does not have a known ownership history, but undocumented sources suggest that this style of cart is German in origin or perhaps merely a style preferred by German settlers.
SIGNE EMMERICH

THE WHEELBARROW

The design of this iron-wheeled box wheelbarrow with stenciled decoration and lightweight frame is typical of those manufactured and sold through catalogs such as Montgomery Ward or Sears, Roebuck in the early twentieth century. This example was reproduced from an original in the Old World Wisconsin collection. An illustration in the 1927 Sears, Roebuck catalog shows a strikingly similar model for sale.
ABOVE: SANDRA MATSON; ABOVE LEFT: ALAN MIRKEN, ED., *1927 EDITION OF THE SEARS, ROEBUCK CATALOGUE* (NEW YORK: CROWN PUBLISHERS, 1970)

The common canal wheelbarrow, also called a railroad barrow, was built primarily for rough use in the trades, but this photograph documents its use on a rural Wisconsin farm in 1906. The open end for side dumping is clearly visible. These boys look as though they are taking a break from the endless chore of chopping firewood. The barrow could easily move the weight of the firewood and most likely served the family well in the garden, too.
WHI IMAGE ID 9821

Fragrant lilacs welcome visitors to the Kristen Pedersen House at Old World Wisconsin just as they did at the home's original Town of Luck location.
SANDRA MATSON

sweet fragrance year after year. After the turn of the century, recently introduced varieties of chrysanthemums and dahlias[15] became popular and joined the delightful array. Little wonder the Danes treasured being in the homes they loved with their family, familiar foods, and colorful flowers.

Kristen Pedersen left Denmark and traveled with his oldest brother and family to join their third brother in Neenah in 1867. The brothers sought affordable land where Danish immigrants with limited financial resources might establish farms of their own. By the 1860s most Wisconsin land considered good for farming had already been claimed. With little money and boundless optimism, the Pedersen brothers found an area in western Wisconsin that reminded them of the beauty of their homeland—except that this land was covered with forest. Those trees would provide timber for building, with the surplus being sold for cash. In 1868 the Pedersens established the community of West Denmark in Polk County. Through the Homestead Act, Kristen Pedersen acquired more than 130 acres in the nearby Town of Luck and began the slow process of clearing land.

Opposite page:
With the addition of a dairy cow, the Danish farm in America felt like home.
LOYD HEATH

Pedersen married Kristiane Christensen, who had emigrated from Norway with her parents and sister in 1869 and settled in Wisconsin, and the Pedersens built a log house in 1872. They oriented the house with the front door facing due north, so that a watch might be set by the sun at noon.[16] There would be no excuse for being late for church or scheduled meetings! They whitewashed interior walls to protect the logs and to add brightness to the rooms.

The slow and arduous land clearing continued. While initially the brothers did all the work by hand, eventually they shared a team of oxen to ease the backbreaking work of hauling trees, pulling stumps, and plowing ground. The oxen also provided transportation.

The Pedersens farmed on a subsistence level. Many immigrant farmers took jobs away from home, especially during winter months, to earn additional income. In wooded areas of northern Wisconsin, lumber camps offered work. But Danish farmers, especially those with children, generally chose not to trade life at home with their families for greater wealth. Self-reliant and frugal, many found local work for lower pay than they could have earned with the lumber industry, or they produced items at home that might be marketed. For example, a Pedersen neighbor carved and sold wooden shoes, which had been found to outlast leather when working in the barnyard. With the addition of a few sheep to the farm, women could knit and then sell warm woolen garments. Cut timber or surplus produce brought in cash, as did the sale of eggs after chickens joined the farm. Kristen Pedersen dug wells by hand and, after adding several milk cows, ran a small dairy farm.

Sadly, Pedersen's wife, Kristiane, passed away a year after they married, shortly after giving birth to their daughter. On a trip to Denmark almost five years later he met Mette Klausen and brought her back to America to be his wife. He lost Mette, too, soon after their second daughter was born. Eventually Kristen's parents came from Denmark to live with him and his girls.[17] The Pedersen household grew limited farm crops, raised their own food, and was content with homemade furnishings. A dog and barn cats shared the family's farm life but stayed outside the house. Domestic pets were not thought clean enough to come inside.[18]

By 1890 the twenty-three and one-half acres Pedersen had cleared included ten in meadow for pasture and hay. On the thirteen cultivated acres, he grew grain, animal feed, and a half acre of potatoes. The family maintained a half-acre kitchen garden, as well.[19] Pedersen never produced the large family workforce needed to operate a thriving farm. He chose to farm at a slow, steady pace and to enjoy the companionship of his family. His daughters fashioned window curtains from flour sacking and cut flowers for the table every day during the growing season,[20] adding coziness and cheer to the family home.

Kristen Pedersen was a fine example of the Danish immigrants who sought freedom and acquired land of their own in Wisconsin. The author of an Old World Wisconsin research report described the conditions Danes such as Pedersen experienced in late-nineteenth-century Polk County:

> *[The] workload [of the Danish immigrants on the farm] was heavy, conditions on the frontier primitive, and eventual economic success a long ways off; and yet they were comfortable in knowing that their farm, hard as it was to develop, was THEIRS. They could cut timber, gather firewood, fish for bullheads, grow a garden, or buy and sell livestock and produce when they wanted to, without having to ask permission of a landlord. This freedom to control their own destiny was something they could never have known as landless laborers in Denmark, but here it was all theirs for the making.*[21]

The Queen of Denmark visited Old World Wisconsin in 1976 to celebrate the restoration of the Kristen Pedersen House, following its relocation from the Town of Luck to Eagle. The yard and kitchen garden have been re-created to enhance the setting for the farmhouse and barn that have been restored to their 1890 appearances.

Fragrant lilac shrubs, drifts of daylilies, and colorful flower beds ringed with rocks frame the doorways to greet visitors. Hollyhocks stand comfortably along the side and rear walls of the dwelling.

The kitchen garden, adjacent to the house, is surrounded on three sides by a vertical board fence. A sidewall of the house provides the fourth wall of the garden enclosure, and bedroom windows offer a lovely peek directly into the garden. Accessible through a gate, a well-defined path invites visitors inside, where they will encounter an interesting selection of vegetables, fruits, and herbs. Laid out in orderly beds, the expected potatoes, beets, carrots, and onions keep company with ruffled blue-green kale and luxuriantly frilly parsley. Colorful cabbages, both red and green, as well as peas, navy beans, celery, cucumbers, and parsnips add to the variety. The tall, ferny foliage of caraway and dill provide visual interest, and their umbels of flowers mature to produce seeds for many culinary possibilities. Cheerful flowers edge the center path, and additional blossoms are scattered among the vegetables. Small fruits fill a portion of the garden space. Harvesting flavorful strawberries, raspberries, and currants is not *all* hard work when sample tastings are permitted.

Beyond the kitchen garden, wild violets and daylilies escape across the landscape, connecting the living space to the meadows and woodlands beyond. This charming setting reminds us of the strong bond the Danes felt with nature, and their pride in creating a happy home life for the family they loved on land they could call their own in this remarkable new country.

Danish Recipes

Previous page:
Beautiful beets, left to right:
Bull's Blood, Golden, and
Chioggia
NANCY L. KLEMP

Opposite page:
Peas
VICK'S FLOWER AND VEGETABLE GARDEN (ROCHESTER, NY: JAMES VICK, 1876)

Pickled Beets *(Syltede Rødbeder)*

This ever-popular sweet-and-sour preparation works well for many root vegetables. Pickling is not just for cucumbers!

Note: Cook beets by cutting off all but 2 inches of beet tops; wash beets and leave whole with root end attached. Cover beets with water and heat to boiling. Simmer until tender, approximately 30 to 40 minutes. Drain and run cold water over beets to cool. Slip skins and remove root ends. Slice thinly for the following recipe.

½ cup white vinegar
½ cup water
½ cup sugar
1 teaspoon salt
⅛ teaspoon pepper
2 cups thinly sliced, freshly cooked beets

Combine vinegar, water, sugar, salt, and pepper in large saucepan. Bring to boil and boil briskly for 2 minutes. Meanwhile, place the sliced beets in a large bowl. Pour the hot marinade over them and let cool uncovered to room temperature.[1]

Pease Porridge

This sometimes did stay in the pot until it was nine days old, as the old nursery rhyme says. In the winter it was frozen with strings in it and then cut into chunks around the strings and carried into the woods by working men who would hang a chunk from a tree until they were ready to build a fire and heat it. *Pease* is an old-fashioned spelling of *peas*.

Melt butter the size of an egg and in it fry 1 onion and ½ head of lettuce. Add 1 tablespoon flour and cook for a few minutes. Add 2½ cups fresh peas (if using dried peas, first soak overnight), 4 cups good chicken stock, and 1 tablespoon sugar. Simmer till peas are tender. Add 1 cup cream and butter the size of a walnut.[2]

Danish Pumpernickel *(Rugbrød)*

Rye meal, ground more coarsely than rye flour, adds texture and character to this traditional Danish rye bread.

4½ teaspoons dry active yeast
1½ cups warm water
½ cup dark molasses
3 tablespoons butter, melted
2 tablespoons caraway seeds
1 teaspoon salt
2 cups rye meal (or cracked wheat)
3 to 4 cups flour

In a large bowl, stir yeast into warm water; let stand 5 minutes to soften. Stir in molasses, butter, caraway seeds, and salt. Stir in rye meal or cracked wheat; let stand 10 minutes. Adding 1 cup at a time, beat in enough flour to make a stiff dough. Turn out onto a lightly floured board. Cover with a dry cloth; let stand 5 to 15 minutes. Wash and grease bowl; set aside. Grease two loaf pans; set aside. Adding flour as necessary, knead dough until smooth, about 10 minutes. Place in greased bowl, turning to grease all sides. Cover and let rise in a warm place until doubled in bulk, about 2 hours. Punch down dough; divide in half. Shape each half into a loaf. Place loaves, seam-side down, in prepared pans. Cover and let rise until doubled in bulk, about 1 hour. Brush tops of loaves with water, then bake 40 to 45 minutes or until loaves sound hollow when tapped with your fingers. Turn out of pans; cool on a rack.[3]

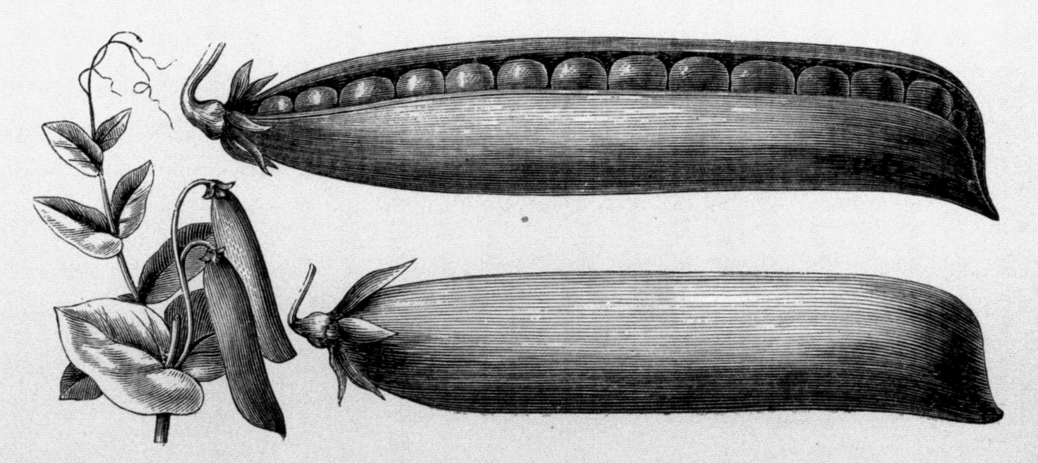

Pork and Cabbage *(Flaesk og Kaal)*

This is a simple, traditional Danish recipe. Remember to simmer gently.

1 small head cabbage
1 pound fresh pork
salt
peppercorns or ground pepper

Slice cabbage thinly and place half in an iron pot with a tight-fitting lid. Slice the pork and salt lightly; layer it evenly over the cabbage. Fill the pot with the remaining cabbage, cover, and simmer very slowly over low heat. A little water may be added, but the dish is better boiled without any, or it loses some flavor. In 2½ to 3 hours the pork should be tender and the cabbage brown. Peppercorns may be added while cooking, or pepper may be served with the meal.[4]

Danish Sugar-Browned Potatoes *(Brunede Kartofler)*

Sugar browning or caramelizing transforms boiled potatoes into something special. Carrots may be prepared in the same manner.

12 small potatoes
boiling salt water (enough to cover potatoes)
¼ cup sugar
¼ cup butter

Cook potatoes in boiling salt water until tender. Drain and peel. Cook sugar in a skillet over low heat, until sugar turns brown. Add butter. Stir constantly until smooth. Add potatoes. Roll potatoes in sugar-butter mixture until coated and golden brown. Serve with pork, poultry, ham, and all meats.[5]

Boiled Red Cabbage *(Rødkaal* or *Rødål)*

This sweet-and-sour dish may be prepared a day ahead and then reheated before serving.

Shred cabbage (approximately 1½ heads) finely and put in a pot with ½ cup cider vinegar. Don't add water. Let simmer for a few hours, till cooked down. Add sugar to taste. Butter and crab apple or red currant jelly may also be added. Continue cooking for another hour or so, stirring occasionally. (Half an hour before cabbage is done, 2 peeled, cored, and chopped apples may also be added.)[6]

Kale in Cream Sauce *(Grønlangkaal)*

Leafy kale is tenderized by cooking and chopping finely before being bathed in cream sauce.

1 pound kale
2 teaspoons salt, divided
4 tablespoons butter
4 tablespoons flour
1 cup milk
1 cup heavy cream
½ teaspoon pepper

Discard tough outer stalks of kale and wash. Tear into large pieces. Place in saucepan with ½ teaspoon salt and just enough cold water to barely cover kale. Cook, covered, over medium heat for 15 minutes or until very tender. Drain kale well and chop fine. In saucepan, melt butter over medium heat; remove from heat and stir in flour. Now add milk and cream all at once, whisking constantly, until sauce comes to a boil and is smooth and thick. Add the remaining 1½ teaspoons of salt, pepper, and chopped kale.[7]

Green Kale Soup

Kale may be freshly harvested from the garden and added directly to the soup kettle. It may also be stored in the root cellar or hung in small bunches to dry for winter use.

½ pound ham or pork hock
2½ quarts water
3 cups coarsely chopped kale
1 medium onion, minced
3 medium potatoes, cubed
3 medium carrots, cubed
flour to thicken
salt and pepper, to taste
whipped cream

Simmer the ham hock in water for 1½ hours. Save the stock. Cook the kale in a separate kettle for 5 minutes and drain it. Add the kale and other vegetables to the cooked ham and stock and cook it until all the vegetables are done, at least 2 hours. Thicken the soup slightly with flour; add salt and pepper. Serve with a dollop of whipped cream.[8]

Kale, also known as borecole

VICK'S FLOWER AND VEGETABLE GARDEN (ROCHESTER, NY: JAMES VICK, 1876)

Apple Cake *(Aeblekage)*

Not really a cake, this classic Danish dessert uses up leftover bread crumbs and may be served with tablespoons of raspberry jam topping the whipped cream.

½ cup butter
1 tablespoon sugar, to taste
2½ cups bread crumbs
4 cups thick, well-flavored applesauce
1 cup heavy cream, whipped and sweetened

Heat butter and stir in sugar. Brown crumbs in mixture until crisp. Place alternate layers of crumbs and applesauce in serving dish, beginning and ending with a layer of crumbs. Chill. Before serving, decorate with swirls of whipped cream. Or place layers in well-buttered baking dish and bake in moderate oven about 45 minutes to 1 hour. Cool and decorate with whipped cream.[9]

Red-Berry Pudding *(Rødgrød)*

Use whatever berries are in season to create this lovely finishing touch to any meal.

1 pound raspberries, strawberries, blackberries, or boysenberries
about 4 cups water
⅓ cup cornstarch
1 cup sugar
pinch of salt
1 cup whipping cream (optional)
¼ cup sliced almonds, toasted (optional)

In medium saucepan, combine berries and water. Bring to a boil. Simmer over low heat 5 minutes. Place a sieve over a medium bowl. Pour berry mixture into sieve; press with the back of a spoon to remove as much pulp as possible. Discard seeds. Measure juice and pulp. If necessary, add water to make 5 cups. In a small bowl, combine cornstarch with ⅔ cups juice from pulp, making a thin paste. Pour remaining juice and pulp into saucepan; bring to a boil over medium heat; stirring occasionally. Stir in sugar, salt, and cornstarch paste. Stirring vigorously with a wooden spoon to keep pudding smooth, cook until thickened. Cover pan; set aside to cool 20 to 30 minutes. Pour cooled pudding into a serving bowl. Top with whipped cream and sprinkle with sliced almonds, if desired. Serve immediately or chill until served.[10]

POLISH SETTLER GARDENS

8

Diligence, Persistence, and Thrift

Nineteenth-century Polish immigrants came to America in search of work. Many carried the dream of earning enough money that they might one day return to their homeland, buy a large farm, and support the family.[1] All sought a chance to earn a decent living. Their lives revolved around their dedication to family, devotion to the Roman Catholic Church, and love of music, dance, and traditional Polish food. Strong, hardworking, and conscientious, they willingly accepted low-level jobs to ensure steady work and regular income. Few spoke English. They found comfort in settling near others who shared their language, religion, and values.

Life in the homeland had been difficult. Political upheavals, economic oppression, and the dwindling availability of farmland brought discouragement. The same blight that had plagued the Irish potato crop hit Poland in the 1840s and 1850s, destroying both food and income. Potatoes supplied a significant portion of the Polish diet. In addition, they constituted the leading cash crop when sold to distilleries for production of the country's most popular drink: vodka. Fortunately, farmers eventually discovered potato varieties less susceptible to the fungal disease.[2]

Although Polish presence in America can be traced back to Jamestown in 1608,[3] large-scale migration of the Poles began in the 1850s. Approximately 90 percent of the Polish people who traveled to America settled in urban areas near plentiful job opportunities, and many purchased homes. Those who chose to farm saved up money to purchase acreage, and many moved to the Midwest.[4] Wisconsin's earliest Polish settlers put down roots near Stevens Point, in Portage County, where they found affordable land available in the late 1850s.[5]

No matter where they settled, each individual contributed support to the family unit. The men traditionally took on the heaviest work. They diligently cut and hauled trees, pulled stumps, and plowed fields. They erected buildings, operated and repaired any farm machinery, and handled working animals—oxen in the early days and eventually horses. In winter, farm men often took jobs in sawmills, in logging camps, or with the railroad to bring in extra income. The women took care of the household, milked cows, fed pigs, and tended poultry as those animals were added to the farm, in addition to maintaining the kitchen garden. Beyond the traditional roles, the Poles were noted for the relative equality of husband and wife. Women frequently worked alongside their men in the fields and had a voice in the financial decisions on the farm.[6] The women sometimes helped with hops and cranberry harvests on nearby farms and brought the additional earned income home to share with the family.[7] Children also contributed. Their work for the family and farm was considered more valuable than schooling. Everyone stayed busy!

Gardens and orchards provided food the family needed to survive. In Wisconsin as in Poland, root crops that could be stored for winter use held particular importance. Most vegetables grew in beds, accessible by paths. Potatoes continued to be a key ingredient in the Polish-American diet. Beets, carrots, celeriac or celery root, root parsley, parsnips, rutabagas, and turnips furnished variety through the long winter months. Horseradish added flavor and cleared the sinuses as a sauce ingredient or grated into soup. The radish, originally cooked as a root vegetable, eventually became a salad ingredient. Onions grew in abundance and flavored many dishes. Cabbage enjoyed huge popularity in soups and stuffings, and as an accompaniment for most meats and other vegetables. Peas, beans, kohlrabi, and lettuce also frequently graced nineteenth-century Polish kitchen gardens and meals. Cucumbers—which in medieval Poland had been eaten fresh and served as fruit and with fruit[8]—gained additional favor pickled.

Celeriac, also known as turnip-rooted celery or celery root and especially popular with nineteenth-century Germans and Poles, adds fine flavor to soups and stews.
VICK'S FLOWER AND VEGETABLE GARDEN, 1876

Kitchen gardens varied in size, from a half acre to several acres, depending on the number of family members. Herbs grew with the vegetables, sometimes snuggled together in the same beds. Dill—for seasoning as well as for pickling—and sweet marjoram—an especially fine ingredient in homemade sausage—brought flavor, fragrance, and beauty to the garden along with chives, caraway, sage, and thyme. Poppies added lovely color and later provided plenty of seed for baking. Mounds of intensely green parsley looked rich and decorative while growing. When cut, they added color and flavor to sauces and numerous other

Previous spread:
The August and Barbara Kruza House, relocated to Old World Wisconsin and restored to its circa 1900 appearance. The stovewood structure combined both agricultural and residential uses under one roof. An interior wall separated the chicken coop—accessible from the door on the left—from the elderly couple's living quarters, which they entered through the door on the right.
SANDRA MATSON

Geraniums brighten the windowsills.
SANDRA MATSON

dishes, eliminated onion on the breath, and aided digestion. Chamomile, mint, and rue sometimes shared garden space.

The home grounds of every self-respecting Pole included flowers. Generally planted near the house or in view from the house, much-loved flowers brightened the work-filled lives of the immigrants and offered a touch of frivolity. Lush roses, sweet lilacs, delicate cornflowers or bachelor's buttons, dancing hollyhocks and sunflowers, shimmering pastel mallows, elegant lilies, fragrant pinks, mignonette, lavender, and lily of the valley enjoyed particular popularity. Housewives generously cut bouquets to grace the church altar or wayside religious shrines.

Fruit provided memories of the Old Country as well as tasty and healthful additions to the diet. Polish-Americans planted berry bushes and were particularly fond of gooseberries, currants, and raspberries. Most farms included rhubarb as well as a small apple orchard of both sweet and tart varieties. Crab apples made delicious jelly.

Potted plants decorated the windowsills. Red, pink, and rose-scented geraniums; fuchsias; myrtles; violets; rosemarys; and begonias all enjoyed popularity. Rosemary and myrtle held special significance, as they shared a long association with Polish wedding traditions. Women eagerly traded seeds and cuttings of favorite plants.

Inside the home, paper flowers made to look like roses, lilacs, morning glories, and other favorites decorated the living space. Often an herb bouquet, gathered and blessed

The leaves of the rose-scented geranium, *Pelargonium graveolens*, are soft textured and fragrant.
VICK'S ILLUSTRATED MONTHLY MAGAZINE 6, 1883

on Assumption Day, was tucked into the frame of a religious picture or woven into a wreath, which was then hung near or over the frame. Polish women took pride in maintaining their homes, no matter how small. Thrifty, enterprising housewives cut patterns in paper to hang in place of costly lace curtains and decorated floors with patterns of colored sand for important holidays.[9] Inspiration came from nature and the flowers and plants these immigrants loved.

Even those who settled in urban areas continued to maintain kitchen gardens. Why would someone spend valuable cash to purchase things that could be grown at home? In the early days, gardens stood in front of the house, as they had in the homeland. Charming mixed beds of vegetables, herbs, and flowers created a cottage garden appearance with pathways for easy access and an inviting bench near the front door. A lovely garden represented the spirit of the housewife, after all—how nice to sit and admire the beauty! When it became apparent that such front yard gardens reflected a peasant status, the kitchen gardens were relocated behind the house. The backyard then became the utilitarian area, home to vegetables and herbs for sustenance with a sprinkling of flowers, surrounded by a fence. Decorative plantings continued in the front, and the bench stayed with them.

August and Barbara Kruza were both on the twilight side of sixty-five years of age when they traveled from Poland to America with two daughters in 1879. Daughter Catherine married Frank Stefaniak, another Polish immigrant. Frank left his twelve-hour-per-day, fourteen-dollar-per-week job in a sugar factory in New York and traveled to Wisconsin with his wife, their young son, and his in-laws with a dream of owning and farming land. They purchased a forty-acre parcel in Hofa Park, Maple Grove Township, near Green Bay in Shawano County and shared a small, one-room log cabin.[10] Hofa Park, established by J. J. Hof, an enterprising Norwegian, advertised land for sale in an established Polish community. Covered with trees and stumps, the "farmland" required laborious cutting and clearing before many crops could be planted. But the land attracted Polish settlement

WATERING-POTS

Virtually all gardeners today use some form of watering or sprinkling can for occasional watering needs. In the nineteenth century these vessels were referred to as "watering-pots." They held anywhere from one to four gallons of water and, while some were made of brass or copper, they were most commonly pieced from tin-plated sheet iron. All these materials are lightweight—an advantage when hand carrying gallons of water from a distance to the garden and a marked improvement over earlier earthenware forms. Tin-plated models were the least expensive but also prone to rust. This shortcoming prompted authors such as Robert Buist in his 1858 publication *The Family Kitchen Gardener* to advise his readers to "keep them well painted, and when not in use, the mouth downwards."[1]

Styles of watering-pots varied but not by much. The basic design consisted of a cylindrical body, applied side and top handles, and a tapering spout, six to eight inches in length. Spouts were fitted with one or more interchangeable rose heads, each pierced with holes, large or small, depending on the plant to be watered: larger holes for durable plants, finer holes for casting a light shower over tender plants. An uncommon form featured an extraordinarily long spout useful when watering plants at a distance from the normal reach of the gardener.

This 1851 illustration captures the characteristic design of nineteenth-century garden watering-pots. The rose head near the pot emphasizes the author's note that "every pot may have several roses pierced with holes of various sizes, to adapt them to different purposes."
P. BARRY, *THE FRUIT GARDEN; A TREATISE* (NEW YORK: CHARLES SCRIBNER, 1851)

The ubiquitous tin-plated watering-pot soon gave way to rust-resistant galvanized steel sprinkling cans, available as early as the 1880s, followed by the amazing functionality of the garden hose. It was the introduction of the garden hose—capable of effortlessly streaming water under pressure—that relegated the watering-pot to spot-watering needs.

During the twentieth century the traditional design and make of watering-pots devolved into extremely lightweight molded-plastic models in an array of garden-bright colors. Time-honored forms in brass, copper, and painted tinplate persist but are priced higher today for their material, their craftsmanship, and perhaps the added cost of bittersweet nostalgia.

NOTE

1. Robert Buist, *The Family Kitchen Gardener* (New York: A. O. Moore, Agricultural Book Publisher, 1858), 12.

WATERING-POTS

Fig. 34.—FRENCH WATERING POT.

Watering-pots sized to hold roughly a gallon of water or less were almost certainly used to water potted plants. The "French Watering Pot," as illustrated and described in the 1868 garden manual *Gardening for the South*, is still being made by hand today. The brass facsimile photographed in use by an Old World Wisconsin interpreter was hand made in Turkey. By using the modern example we can determine if "by the peculiar construction of the handle, the weight is more easily balanced in the hands, which enables the user to empty with far less muscular exertion than with a pot upon the old plan," as the author claimed in 1868.

WILLIAM WHITE, *GARDENING FOR THE SOUTH* (NEW YORK: ORANGE JUDD AND CO., 1868); PHOTO: NANCY L. KLEMP

Fig. 33.—WATERING POT.

The design for this long-spouted watering-pot was extrapolated from the 1868 illustration of the same. Whenever possible, Old World Wisconsin captures variety in the design of the simplest forms of cultural material to enliven its hands-on living history program.

WILLIAM WHITE, *GARDENING FOR THE SOUTH* (NEW YORK: ORANGE JUDD AND CO., 1868); PHOTO: NANCY L. KLEMP

WATERING-POTS

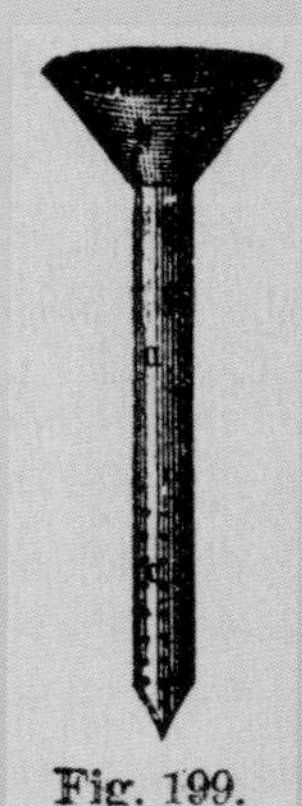

Fig. 199.

The ubiquitous watering-pot was not necessarily the sole watering implement used in the nineteenth-century kitchen garden. A made-on-the-farm water barrel cart or purchased garden engine (see page 16) could be employed to distribute large quantities of water onto the garden beds. Specialized watering needs such as how to deliver water directly to a plant's root system, prompted the clever design of thrifty tools like the watering tube.

A recurring theme in nineteenth-century garden manuals is an emphasis on thrift and household economy. Authors frequently promoted the design of garden implements that could be made on the farm by a crafty farmer or with the aid of a local tradesman. A good example is this tin watering tube, illustrated and described in *Farm Appliances and How to Make Them*, an 1887 practical handbook for the farm. This was not a homemade version of a factory-made device available for sale elsewhere but a truly one-of-a-kind tool used for deep watering. The instructions note: "Any local tinsmith can make the tube at a slight expense." Above its sealed tip, the tube is pierced with several rows of small holes. Water poured into the funnel seeps out through the holes reaching deep under the soil, saturating a plant's root system. Several of these tubes were made following the published pattern and put to the test in Old World Wisconsin's gardening program.

GEORGE A. MARTIN, *FARM APPLIANCES AND HOW TO MAKE THEM* (NEW YORK: ORANGE JUDD AND CO., 1887), REPRINT (NEW YORK: LYONS PRESS, 1997); PHOTO: NANCY L. KLEMP

The chickens that lived under the same roof as August and Barbara Kruza provided a steady supply of eggs for kitchen use.
SANDRA MATSON

Opposite page: Barred Plymouth Rock chickens were a popular Midwestern breed in the late nineteenth century and are among the historic breeds at Old World Wisconsin.
THE *NEBRASKA FARMER*, APRIL 2, 1896, CITED IN PAUL C. JOHNSON, *FARM ANIMALS IN THE MAKING OF AMERICA* (DES MOINES, IA: WALLACE HOMESTEAD BOOKS, 1975); BOTTOM PHOTO: LOYD HEATH

and offered the immigrants comfort in a community of fellow countrymen, and the eventual construction of a Catholic church pleased people tremendously.

The Stefaniak family grew, and eventually Frank built separate lodgings on the same property for his in-laws. The Kruzas lived spartanly in a one-room home of stovewood construction. The stovewood building style was not known in Poland, where tight-fitting, squared-timbered log homes were the norm. Evidently the technique of laying cordwood pieces into a bed of mortar was developed in Upper Midwestern America or Canada and was readily adopted by Poles and other immigrant groups.[11]

With the chicken coop housed under the same roof as the Kruzas, gathering eggs could hardly be more convenient. Divided by an interior wall, the two sections were accessed by separate entry doors, with the chickens on the left side of the building and the couple on the right. Living near their daughter and her family, and within a largely Polish community, the Kruzas never learned to speak English. They enjoyed their independence and the company and assistance of their family.

Many retired Poles maintained their own gardens for as long as they were able. Often, aging parents and their children worked out agreements guaranteeing support for the elders throughout their lifetime in exchange for the transfer of title to the property; a legally binding "life lease" or "bond of support" frequently recorded the details agreed upon.

FIRST PRIZE BREEDING PEN,
AT NEW YORK - 1895
OWNED BY
A · C · HAWKINS
LANCASTER · MASS ·
FIRST PRIZE BREEDING PEN OF B. P. ROCKS AT MADISON SQUARE GARDEN, NEW YORK, OWNED BY A. C. HAWKINS, LANCASTER, MASS.

Beds of tasty vegetables. Garden publications in the 1880s recommended planting petunias with potatoes to repel potato beetles.

ABOVE: NANCY L. KLEMP; RIGHT: SANDRA MATSON

A sampling of lifetime support agreements from late-nineteenth and early-twentieth-century Shawano County indicate that retirement kitchen gardens ranged in size from two rods by three rods (approximately thirty feet by fifty feet) to two acres, with a half acre most common. In addition, the children often promised to provide designated quantities of meat, produce, additional kitchen staples, soap, firewood, a number or percentage of the farm's livestock, etc. Potatoes and cabbage dominated the vegetable lists, with rutabagas, carrots, peas, and onions following behind in lesser quantities.[12] Aging Poles continued to prefer the traditional diet of their homeland.

The Shawano County home of August and Barbara Kruza was relocated to Old World Wisconsin in 1989 and restored to its circa 1900 appearance. The re-created kitchen garden, conveniently located just steps from the house and enclosed by a chicken wire fence, features rectangular beds of vegetables and herbs, with a sprinkling of flowers. Chamomile promises blossoms for soothing tea. Pastel flowers of vining petunias weave their way through beds of potatoes, pleasing people with sweet fragrance while also repelling potato beetles. The quilted texture of the savoy cabbages have a dressed-up appearance when compared to the smooth leaves of the common cabbage varieties, all greatly enjoyed in Polish cuisine. Celeriac with celery-flavored roots; earthy, deep-red beets; sweet, crunchy carrots; and piquant onions join other traditionally Polish crops in the garden and the kitchen.

More favorite flowers and herbs grow in a small bed in the front yard. Perennial lavenders, lilies, mallows, pinks, bleeding hearts, and rue mingle with seasonal additions such as geraniums, mignonette, myrtle, and rosemary.

Nineteenth-century Polish immigrants never shunned hard work. They endured physical drudgery from factories to farmland, forging promising futures for themselves and their families. They lived frugally and worked diligently. Inspired by nature, they loved flowers, bright colors, hearty Polish food, music, and dancing, and they enjoyed life. Poles who settled in America brought many traditions with them from the Old Country, and their zest for life continues. When speaking of her heritage, a twentieth-century Polish immigrant explains, "Without music, without flowers, without our past, we don't exist."[13]

Polish Recipes

Previous page: Assorted heirloom potatoes: Bintje, Garnet Chile, Irish Cobbler, and Russet Burbank
SANDRA MATSON

Opposite page: Portly pigs
TRANSACTIONS OF THE WISCONSIN STATE AGRICULTURAL SOCIETY, 1886

Barley Soup *(Krupnik)*

Soup is traditionally a fundamental part of a Polish dinner and begins the meal. *Krupnik* is tasty and nourishing enough to serve as the main course. Pork or lean smoked bacon may be substituted for the beef. Bread is not necessarily served with a Polish dinner.

Pour 3½ pints water over 1 pound of beef and 1 pound of beef bones cut into small pieces and cook over low heat. After 1 hour add mixed vegetables (carrots, parsley, celeriac root, leek, and 1 onion) and 4 small dried mushrooms. When the meat turns tender, put the broth through a sieve. Cut the meat into cubes and the vegetables and mushrooms into thin strips.

Cook ¾ pint of the cooked broth, salted to taste, with 4 to 6 ounces pearl barley to make kasha.[1] When the kasha is cooked, add 1 tablespoon butter and mix the kasha for a while with a wooden spoon, until it turns white.

Add the cooked kasha to the remaining broth and after adding 3 potatoes diced into cubes, cook for a further 15 to 20 minutes. Now add the diced meat, mushrooms, and vegetables to the broth and salt to taste. Sprinkle with minced parsley before serving.[2]

Pork Roast with Caraway Polish Style

Many nineteenth-century Wisconsin farmers raised pigs to supply meat for the table. The seasonings in this pork recipe lend it a distinctively Polish flair.

Buy 2 pounds fine pork, cut into a cube, with the skin. Make shallow incisions in the skin with a sharp knife in a checkerboard pattern. Rub the meat with salt, a large pinch of [sweet] marjoram, and a heaped teaspoon of caraway an hour before roasting. In a cast-iron pan heat intensely 1½ ounces lard; add meat and brown it on all sides. Place the browned meat with the skin-side down and add 2 sliced onions and some boiling water (or broth, if available). During roasting replenish the evaporated liquid from time to time. After 30 minutes of roasting in a hot oven, turn the roast over so that the skin is on top and continue roasting, basting it with its own sauce from time to time. The incisions in the skin will spread out forming an appetizing checkerboard.

Cut the ready roast into thin slices and pour the roast sauce with the onion over it.[3]

LOU BURK DEL
BREEDER'S GAZETTE SC.

Savoy cabbage wears beautifully quilted leaves and is especially fine flavored.
NANCY L. KLEMP

Kapusta

Fresh cabbage is combined with sauerkraut for a creative spin on a vegetable popular with Polish immigrants.

1 onion, sliced or chopped
2 tablespoons bacon fat
1½ to 2 pounds sauerkraut, rinsed
1 small head cabbage, finely shredded
2 cups water
2 tablespoons brown sugar
salt and pepper, to taste

Saute onion in bacon fat. Add sauerkraut and top with fresh cabbage. Add water, sugar, salt, and pepper. Simmer 2 hours.[4]

Cucumber Salad Polish Style *(Mizeria)*

Fresh dill weed is added to a creamy sweet-and-sour dressing to create a refreshing cucumber salad.

Peel young cucumbers with small seeds and shred them thinly. Sprinkle with a teaspoon of salt and squeeze out lightly after a few minutes.

The dressing is made with cream: for each ½ cup sour cream add the juice of ½ lemon, ½ teaspoon castor sugar and, if necessary, a little salt and a copious teaspoon of finely minced dill. Dust the *mizeria* with ¼ teaspoon ground pepper. Mix and place in a cool place half an hour before serving.[5]

Pierogi with Cabbage Filling *(Pierożki z Kapustą)*

Pierogi are boiled or baked dumplings. They may be savory—filled with cabbage, cheese, or meat—or prepared with a sweet filling of berries, cherries, or apples for a delightful dessert.

PIEROGI:

4 cups flour
1 teaspoon salt
4 eggs
1 cup cold water

Combine flour and salt in a large bowl. Cut in eggs with pastry blender, one at a time. Add water, ¼ cup at a time. Blend well. Knead on a floured board until dough is elastic. Let rest under a bowl for 30 minutes.

Divide into 3 or 4 portions and roll out as needed on a floured board as for pie crust. Cut 3-inch circles (using a glass with rim dipped in flour) and place 1 tablespoon (or more) of filling on one side. Fold over to form a half-circle; moisten edges with water and seal well.

Drop pierogi, a few at a time, into large kettle of salted boiling water; when they rise to the surface, remove with slotted spoon and drain well on a cake rack set over a large roasting pan; remove to buttered waxed paper; do not stack.

To serve, fry until crisp in half shortening and half butter. Or saute onions in butter, then add pierogi and cover.

CABBAGE FILLING:

1 large cabbage
1 medium onion, chopped
butter
salt and pepper, to taste

Quarter cabbage and remove core. Boil until tender and drain well; chop as for coleslaw. Press out as much liquid as possible. Saute onion in butter until well browned. Add cabbage; stir and fry until almost dry. Season to taste. Cool before using to fill pierogi.[6]

Versatile cabbage, a favorite vegetable of the Poles, finds itself a valued ingredient in countless recipes.
GERALD H. EMMERICH JR.

Christmas Poppy-Seed Cake

Christmas poppy-seed cake showcases the seed from the silky-petaled poppy flowers. This recipe is special and extravagant—but then Christmas is celebrated only once a year.

YEAST CAKE:

This is prepared from 6 ounces butter, 6 ounces castor sugar, 2 whole eggs (or 1 egg and 2 egg yolks), a pinch of salt, 1½ ounces yeast, ½ cup milk, 12 ounces wheat flour, and 1 egg white. Cream the butter with the sugar and, when well blended, gradually add the following ingredients: the eggs, salt, and the yeast dissolved in lukewarm milk. Finally, add the flour and knead the dough well by hand. After kneading, the dough should be allowed to rise (covered with a cloth) for not less than an hour. After this, roll out the dough thinly on a floured board, shaping it into a rectangle; cover with egg white (so that the filling does not separate from the cake) and spread filling evenly. Roll the cake up tightly, pressing well on the ends, not rolling them under.

The poppy-seed cake thus prepared should rise before baking in a buttered pan. The baking time is 45 to 50 minutes.

After baking and cooling, the cake may be covered with lemon icing and, before the icing sets, sprinkled with finely chopped, lightly browned almonds.

POPPY-SEED FILLING:

Pour 1¾ pints boiling milk over 1 pound poppy seeds that have been washed. Cook (the milk should barely simmer) over low heat for 30 minutes. Drain the poppy seeds in a sieve and put through a meat grinder (use the finest sieve) 3 to 4 times.

In a cast-iron pot melt 6 ounces butter and ¾ cup honey; add a finely ground vanilla bean, 4 ounces not too finely ground almonds (or other nuts), 6 ounces raisins and ½ cup finely chopped candied orange peel. Now add the poppy seeds and fry together with the above ingredients for 15 minutes (mixing often to avoid burning). Cool the mixture slightly and add 3 to 4 egg yolks, well beaten with a cup of sugar. Add the remaining egg whites, beaten stiffly. The flavor will be even more elegant if a brandy-glass of good rum or cognac is added. The filling is ready. Spread it on the cake while still lukewarm.[7]

FINNISH SETTLER GARDENS

9

An Entrepreneurial Spirit

Finnish immigrants came to America in the second half of the nineteenth century in search of independence, with a desire to shape their own destinies and with the hope of land ownership. Hardworking and honest, reputedly having "the strength of a bear [and] the endurance of a mule,"[1] most arrived with little money and found jobs as low-paid unskilled laborers. Employers sought the sober and industrious Finns for work in mines, quarries, tanneries, factories, railroads, and logging camps as well as at sea. Many who formerly farmed in Finland worked a succession of jobs in the New World, restless to find a piece of property to settle and farm—and to call home.

In the late 1880s numerous Finns found inexpensive land still available in northwestern Wisconsin. Nearby Michigan and Minnesota were already home to sizable Finnish populations. Experienced in dealing with the challenges of the northern climate and difficult terrain in their homeland, the hardy immigrants tackled the Wisconsin "cutover" and made a valiant effort to turn it into profitable farmland. With much acreage previously harvested by the loggers, the remaining poor soil, scrubby underbrush, and naked stumps held little appeal to most immigrant groups. The persevering Finns doggedly began clearing the land and establishing their new homes.

The small, rectangular log houses the settlers built on their new land in northern Wisconsin exemplified the Scandinavian understanding of and familiarity with wood. Snugly fit logs kept out the draft, and a flat-pitched roof held snow for insulation in the northern climate. (Interestingly, the Finns first introduced the log cabin to America during early colonization in the seventeenth century when they demonstrated laying logs horizontally rather than vertically in a stockade-like configuration.)

The slow, exhausting work of clearing land for planting—typically at the rate of one to three acres per year—made the reality of actually raising crops a long way off.

Previous spread: Rutabagas in the kitchen garden at the Heikki and Maria Ketola Farm, re-created at Old World Wisconsin.
TERRY MOLTER

Milk cows at the Ketola Farm
LOYD HEATH

Men could fish, hunt, and trap for food, but they needed cash for tools and supplies to begin farming. The incentives to earn additional income burned especially strong because most Finns came to America alone, leaving their families behind in the Old Country. Many men sought work away from their land for part of the year to earn money for the family's passage.

Lack of land, overpopulation, poor economic conditions, high rates of unemployment, periods of bad weather leading to famine and starvation, political unrest—the reasons for leaving Finland far outweighed any arguments to stay. Families waited for their tickets to America. As soon as the entire family arrived, they all worked together to prepare the land for planting. Men concentrated on fieldwork while women tended to the households. Children helped with chores. As soon as they could afford it, Finnish immigrants added a milk cow or two to their farmsteads, and the care of these animals became the wife's responsibility.

The family also worked together in the kitchen garden, which revolved around root crops. Potatoes made up the largest percentage, constituting at least half and sometimes up to seven-eighths of the garden! Rutabagas also grew in large quantities. Chopped or sliced and served in water to livestock, rutabagas earned a reputation for improving the milk production of dairy cows. Frugal Finns found many ways to prepare the "Swede turnip" for human consumption as well. Other popular vegetables included turnips, beets, carrots, and onions. Sometimes peas, beans, cabbage, and cucumbers joined the selection.

An enticing advertisement printed in *Wisconsin Farmers' Institutes: A Hand-Book of Agriculture*, 1896

FARM LANDS. TIMBER LANDS.

NORTHERN WISCONSIN.

Chicago & North-Western Railway Co.'s

LANDS

A large tract of lands, heavily timbered with Maple, Birch, Basswood, Elm and Hemlock, suitable for agricultural purposes, convenient to thriving cities and villages, which make for the settler a ready cash market for his telegraph poles, posts, cordwood and logs, which he cuts in clearing his farm, thus enabling him with a small capital to make himself a home. Farm produce finds a ready market at milling and mining towns close at hand.

Dairying is carried on with success in Langlade and Shawano Counties.

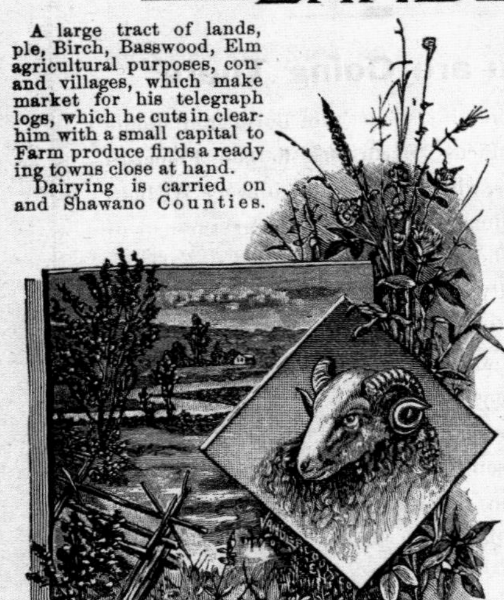

The soil is well adapted to raising the best quality of grasses; water is abundant and pure.

Langlade County is particularly well adapted to general farming; all grasses, oats, wheat, rye, barley, corn, potatoes and all root crops yield large returns.

Shawano County is well adapted to general farming and sheep raising.

This part of Wisconsin is no longer remote from markets, as the railroads leading into the mining and lumbering district furnish a ready market for all produce.

These lands are for sale on long time, easy terms and low rate of interest to actual settlers.

School accommodation is good and ample; Taxes low: Climate healthful; No Blizzards; No Droughts.

Timber for manufacturing is unlimited and of the best quality for Stave, Heading and Hoop Factories, Furniture Factories, Saw Mills, Pulp Mills and Tanneries.

Apply to

C. E. SIMMONS,
Land Commissioner, CHICAGO, ILL.

C. S. PIERCE,
General Land Agent, MILWAUKEE, WIS.

Mention "Farmers' Institute Bulletin" when writing to advertisers.

290

An 1885 lithograph of loggers at work

VICK'S ILLUSTRATED MONTHLY MAGAZINE 8, 1885

A Finnish kitchen garden re-created at Old World Wisconsin's Ketola Farm. Potato plants are in the foreground.
TERRY MOLTER

Rutabagas provided food for livestock as well as for families.
TERRY MOLTER

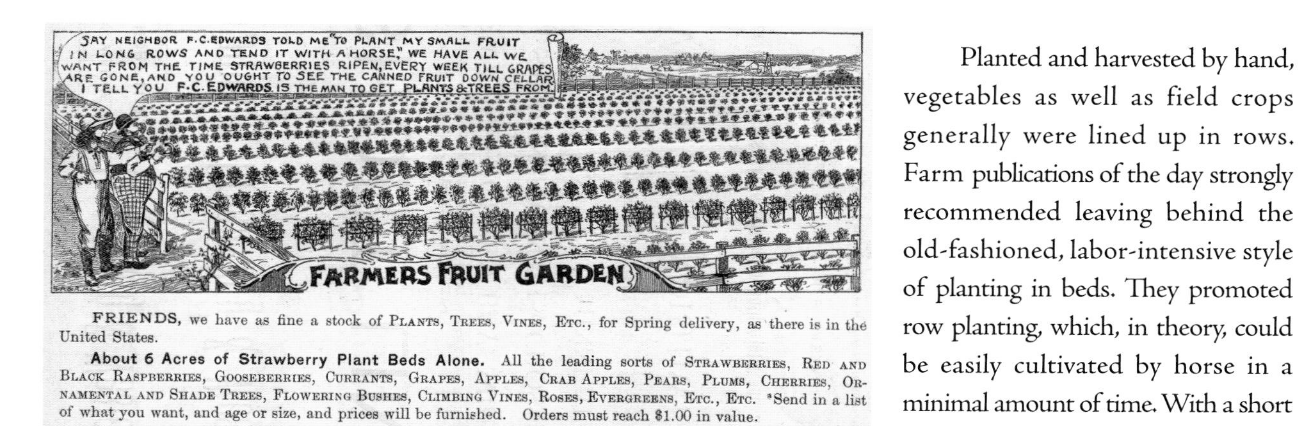

A late-nineteenth-century Wisconsin farm publication recommended planting in rows rather than beds.
WISCONSIN FARMERS' INSTITUTES: A HAND-BOOK OF AGRICULTURE, 1896

Planted and harvested by hand, vegetables as well as field crops generally were lined up in rows. Farm publications of the day strongly recommended leaving behind the old-fashioned, labor-intensive style of planting in beds. They promoted row planting, which, in theory, could be easily cultivated by horse in a minimal amount of time. With a short growing season and long winters, the family worked diligently to store food in the root cellar to provide winter meals. Food tended to be basic and bland. Finns boast of using only salt and pepper for seasonings. In checking nineteenth-century recipes, it seems caraway, dill, parsley, and thyme occasionally snuck into the garden.

Many Finnish-American families also planted small apple orchards. Apples could be enjoyed in pastries and other tasty treats or sliced and strung to dry for future use. Wild fruits such as raspberries, strawberries, cranberries, and plums became jams and jellies, sauces, syrups, and juices. Currants and gooseberries, familiar from Finland, eventually joined the plantings. Cows produced the milk that was used to make buttermilk, butter, cream, and cheese. Homegrown grains became bread or porridge, and delicious baked goods served with morning coffee always received a warm welcome. With the addition of meat and fish, some rice for pudding, and the ever-present and much-loved coffee, housewives could prepare the traditional meals of their homeland.

Flowers rarely enjoyed gardens of their own. In Finland, where farmers struggled for survival, decorative gardens had been considered a useless luxury. Feeling a deep connection with trees and woods, Finnish immigrants believed that nothing could compete with the beauty of nature. Tucked into natural settings, orange and white lilies, fragrant lilacs and lily of the valley, wild pansies or Johnny-jump-ups, and sweet roses sometimes enhanced the landscape. Portulacas or moss roses and sweet William were easily sprinkled where they could be admired. Occasionally brilliant blue cornflowers or bachelor's buttons, fondly remembered waving in fields of grain in the Old Country, found their way into the Finnish-American home grounds. Treasured houseplants included geraniums, myrtles, fuchsias, and begonias.[2]

THE KETOLA ROOT CELLAR

It is difficult to comprehend challenges faced by nineteenth-century rural farm families in their efforts to preserve fruits and vegetables to last the winter or keep milk products fresh without the aid of refrigeration. For centuries and across cultures, perishable foods have been canned, dried, preserved in vinegar brine through a process called pickling, or made into sauces and jams for table use in winter. Long-term preservation of whole vegetables and fruits in their natural state, however, requires a controlled environment that is both dry and capable of maintaining a consistently cool temperature. That was the purpose of a well-designed root cellar.

Dug out from the side of a hill and with heavy earthen walls on three sides, this style of root cellar was a common one in northern Wisconsin.
ELLEN PENWELL

Conditions that cause vegetables and fruits to decay are moisture and heat, or frequent and extreme changes in temperature such as alternating freezing and thawing. A root cellar built below the home or as a separate structure provided a level of protection. Among Finnish settlements in northern Wisconsin, a prevalent form of root cellar was an underground chamber dug out from the side of a hill.[1] The chamber door was flush with the side of the hill, but the cellar sides and back wall extended into the hill, buried under three or four feet of dirt. The cavelike interior was sided with cedar logs, adding to the thickness of the natural wall to exclude frosts. The room was ventilated through the dirt ceiling. This provided air circulation, prevented mold growth, and vented gases produced by the stored crops such as ethylene gas, which hastens ripening and, eventually, spoilage. An exterior front door opened into a small entryway that offered further insulation by means of a second door leading into the cellar interior. A good root cellar maintained a cool but not freezing temperature year-round.

A root cellar similar in design to that just described was built at Old World Wisconsin to complement the museum's 1915 Finnish farmstead. This exhibit represents the Heikki and Maria Ketola farm, originally located in the Town of Oulu, Bayfield County. Heikki Ketola's largest root crop in 1915 was one acre of rutabagas grown primarily as feed for his milk cows. Rutabagas, a traditional food in the Finnish diet, were also sown in quantity in the kitchen garden for domestic use along with potatoes, onions, beets, turnips, and carrots. All these foods would

THE KETOLA ROOT CELLAR

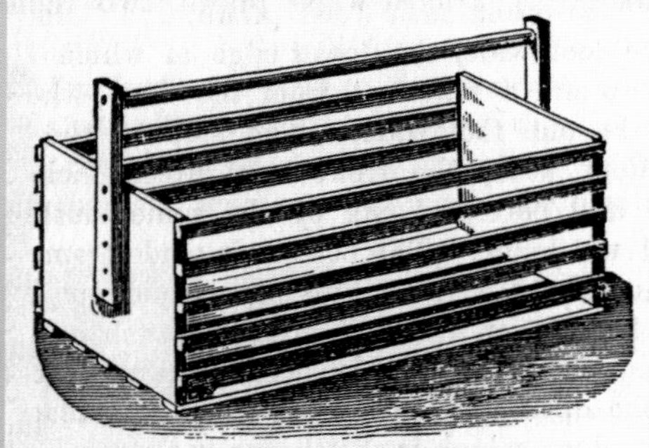

Fig. 116.—CONVENIENT BARN BASKET.

Gathered produce ready to be stored in the Ketola root cellar. The handled "barn baskets" seen here were made following directions published in *Farm Conveniences: Practical Handbook for the Farm*. The instructions stressed the value of making the baskets in three sizes: one bushel, half bushel, and a peck. When crates were sized to a known measure, home gardeners could gather and calculate their harvest at the same time. The two unhandled crates pictured near the cellar doorway are designed to be stacked. Note how their slatted construction provides necessary ventilation.

FARM CONVENIENCES: PRACTICAL HANDBOOK FOR THE FARM (NEW YORK: ORANGE JUDD CO., 1900), REPRINT BY DENIS BOYLES (NEW YORK: THE LYONS PRESS, 1998); PHOTO: GERALD H. EMMERICH JR.

have wintered in the root cellar, with the largest yields—rutabagas and potatoes—stored in open bins and the remainder stored in any number of stackable wooden crates. Ketola's large harvest of rutabagas grown for animal feed was probably buried in pits in the field or mounded near the barn, reserving the root cellar for family use and the storage of seeds that were the hope and promise of the next year's harvest.[2] Crated apples, jugs of apple cider vinegar, canned fruits and vegetables, crocks of lard, and canned, salted, and pickled meats also wintered in the root cellar. During the summer months, the root cellar functioned like our modern-day refrigerator, keeping easily spoiled products such as milk, cream, yogurt, cheese, and butter at a cool temperature between mealtimes.

NOTES

1. Unpublished research report, "Root Cellar," by Nancy C. Payne, Old World Wisconsin, August 1972, and unpublished field notes by Alan Pape, restoration superintendent, Old World Wisconsin, May 1975.

2. Getto, Oscar. Interview with Gary Payne, November 4, 1974. Old World Wisconsin. Oscar Getto was one of Heikki and Maria Ketola's sons.

Maria Ketola feeding the family's calves in the Town of Oulu. Finnish women traditionally tended to the dairy cows.
WHI IMAGE ID 76705

The Jacob and Louisa Rankinen House, restored to its 1897 appearance at Old World Wisconsin, and re-created kitchen garden. The Rankinens and other farmers struggled to raise enough food to survive in the northern Wisconsin cutover region.
LARRY DICKERSON

Never ostentatious, the Finns preferred neatness and cleanliness on their farms, in their homes, and in their personal hygiene. Each household included a separate sauna or bathhouse, and family members bathed on Saturdays. On issues of health, they favored vigorous exercise and healthful eating over patent medicines.[3]

They remained busy during the long winter months. Women enjoyed weaving and knitting garments and rugs, using wool from their own sheep. Men employed their craftsmanship with wood to fashion skis, snowshoes, and assorted household items as needed. Frequently the men took jobs away from the farm for weeks at a time to bring home some much-needed cash.

Through years of struggle and under challenging conditions the Finnish immigrants persevered. They sought the company of other Finns through their community Lutheran churches and various social organizations. They supported education for their children. Adults, too, continued to value learning; they read widely and sought information to make improvements on their farms. Finnish immigrants found land ownership and independence attainable in the rugged northwestern Wisconsin cutover. Although it had been a lengthy struggle for them, their hard-earned new homes were worth the journey.

When recalling an incredible series of hardships and disasters encountered through the years since leaving her beloved Finland—including decades living in northern Wisconsin—one courageous and resourceful woman expressed the attitude prevalent in the Finnish-American community: "Although life in the wilderness was simple and we had only the bare necessities of life, life was, however, enjoyable, for joy is not in the plentitude of possessions but in the state of mind."[4] She also wrote, "I have often thought that those that never encounter any adversity do not know what joy is."[5]

Jacob Rankinen left his wife, Louisa, and two children in Finland in the mid-1880s while he worked on British sailing vessels for several years. Difficult conditions in the homeland forced many Finns to look outside their own country to earn money to support their families. Rankinen "jumped ship" along the California coast and worked his way east. He found employment with the railroad, spent some time as a fisherman in Duluth, Minnesota, and then worked in the iron mines and as a carpenter in Ironwood, Michigan. He opened a boarding house in Ironwood and in 1888 sent passage money home. His family joined him, and they soon added two more children.

In 1891 Rankinen went off to Wisconsin, where he filed a homestead claim on eighty acres in the Town of Oulu, Bayfield County, near a settlement of other Finns. At long last, he could own land and put down roots. The family settled there together in 1892.[6]

The Rankinens operated a subsistence-level farm and managed to add about two newly cleared and planted acres of land each year. They grew hay, oats, and rutabagas for livestock feed. The family worked together and raised most of what they needed to get by. Some chickens and a few milk cows brought income from the sale of surplus eggs and butter. One sheep provided wool for warm clothing and rugs. Possessing considerable carpentry and blacksmithing skills, Rankinen proved capable of building and repairing as needs arose on his farm.[7]

A half-acre kitchen garden planted to potatoes, rutabagas, and small quantities of beets, carrots, turnips, and onions provided limited variety but welcome nourishment for the family. Root crops carefully stored in the cellar ensured year-round food availability. The family harvested apples from their small orchard and picked wild plums and berries.[8]

The Rankinens enjoyed participating in and supporting the area's Finnish community. At times their family home served as both a schoolhouse and a site for religious services until dedicated buildings could be erected—with the help of Rankinen labor.[9]

The Rankinen family worked hard and had little material wealth, but they found fulfillment in the lives they made for themselves.

Heikki Ketola also endured a lengthy separation from family in his quest for a better life. He left his wife, Maria, and five children in Finland when he headed for America in 1889. After working as a longshoreman and living in Ohio for two years, he traveled to northern Wisconsin. In 1892 he entered a homestead claim on forty acres in what would become the Town of Oulu, Bayfield County; built a small log house; and set about clearing land.[10] He hunted and trapped game for food and sought outside work to earn cash for a period of weeks or months each year. Working alone, Ketola managed to clear the trees, stumps, brush, and stones from about one acre of his property annually.[11]

In 1898, almost ten years after he left for America, Ketola sent money for his patient wife and children in Finland to join him. He established a small farm and soon recognized the importance of diversification and education as well as the value of staying current with improving agricultural technology. The family continued to work hard. Over the years they built a successful dairy operation and grew red clover, which had been recently recommended by the University of Wisconsin College of Agriculture for its value as animal feed and for its ability to increase soil fertility,[12] as well as oats and rutabagas for animal feed. Ketola also capitalized on his outgoing personality and found

Maria and Heikki Ketola with three of their children, Town of Oulu
WHI IMAGE ID 74635

he had a knack for salesmanship. He ran a general store out of the family kitchen, eventually selling telephones, DeLaval cream separators, and John Deere equipment, and became an agent for the Bush Motor Car Company. Fortunately, he finally built an additional structure to serve as the store![13]

While his business ventures grew successful, the family never lived extravagantly. A skilled craftsman, Ketola hand made numerous items for the household, including kitchen benches, cupboards, brooms, and baskets. His wife, Maria, wove rugs on a borrowed loom and made quilts and warm socks and sweaters of wool from their sheep. Both held conservative religious beliefs and forbade dancing and drinking in the household.

The Ketola family successfully combined traditions of their Finnish homeland with entrepreneurial American opportunities. They maintained an acre of vegetables,[14] focusing on the traditional Finnish favorites. Potatoes and rutabagas, of course, occupied most of the garden space. Beets, carrots, peas, and beans[15] added some variety to meals and could be stored for winter use. By 1915 a half-acre apple orchard supplied the family with fruit for pastries, desserts, sauces, and occasional flavorful accompaniments in meat and vegetable dishes.[16]

Opposite page, clockwise: Maria Ketola greets visitors to her home in Bayfield County.
OLD WORLD WISCONSIN RESEARCH FILE

The Heikki and Maria Ketola House at Old World Wisconsin, which has been restored to its 1915 appearance.
SANDRA MATSON

Lilacs added sweet fragrance and charm to the homesteads of early settlers.
TERRY MOLTER

Old World Wisconsin's Finnish farm exhibits revolve around the former Bayfield County homes of Jacob and Louisa Rankinen and Heikki and Maria Ketola. Both log homes provide examples of the Finns' superb craftsmanship in working with wood as they created architectural styles familiar from their homeland.

The one-and-a-half-story log structure covered with vertical plank siding that Rankinen built shows a house style that had fairly recently been introduced in late-nineteenth-century Finland. Interestingly, all materials used in the house's original construction came from his Town of Oulu farm, with the exception of the windows, chimney brick, and door hardware.[17]

The large re-created kitchen garden, located near the house and situated on a plot of ground cleared of trees, is planted with row after row of Finnish staples. Potatoes and rutabagas dominate, and carrots, beets, turnips, and onions—other common root crops that store well to provide sustenance year-round—struggle to flourish in the sandy soil reminiscent of that found in northwestern Wisconsin. Smaller amounts of beans, peas, cabbage, cucumbers, dill, caraway, and parsley complete the selection. Not the least bit frivolous, the garden offers a scaled-down example of a typical late-nineteenth-century Finnish-American utilitarian kitchen garden in northern Wisconsin.

The low-profile, one-story Heikki and Maria Ketola House, with its flat-pitched roof to hold snow in winter for insulation from the cold, is an example of a traditional building style of long standing in Finland. Ladders alongside the dwelling and visible on the roof—another carryover from the homeland—provided easy roof access in the event of a dreaded chimney fire. A root cellar, popular prior to refrigeration as a place to store food, is built into a hillside behind the house.

The kitchen garden located to the side of the family home is, as with the Rankinen garden, laid out in rows rather than beds for ease of mechanical cultivation if desired. Most Finnish-American kitchen gardens in northern Wisconsin apparently continued to be sources of food only, and they remained largely unadorned. While lilacs, daylilies, and lily of the valley frame the front of the Ketola house with color and fragrance, the only decorative touches in the kitchen garden are brushstrokes of vivid blue cornflowers, reminders of flowers that grew in fields of the Old Country. In northern Wisconsin, Finnish-Americans could look upon the land they had worked so diligently to clear and plant and proudly call it their own.

Finnish Recipes

Finnish Barley Pudding *(Uunipuuro)*

The Finnish country tradition of eating homegrown grains in the form of gruels and puddings dates back many centuries. The pudding may even be served with hot milk as a lunch or supper dish.

1¼ cups large-grain barley
4 cups water
6 cups boiling milk
⅓ cup butter

Soak barley in water overnight or for several hours. Cook in the water. As barley begins absorbing water, gradually add boiling milk, stirring constantly. Cook barley over lowest possible heat for about 30 minutes. Stir frequently to prevent scorching. Transfer barley to buttered 1½- or 2-quart baking dish. Dot with butter and bake until golden brown, about 2 hours.[1]

Rye-Meal Bread *(Ruisleipä)*

Bread was considered a mainstay of the Finnish diet; a meal without bread was incomplete. Rye meal lends the flavor and nutrition of whole rye grain in this traditional Finnish bread. Preheat the oven to 375 degrees before baking.

2¼ teaspoons dry yeast
2 teaspoons sugar
1¼ cups warm water
1½ teaspoons salt
2 tablespoons melted shortening
1½ cups rye meal
1¾ to 2 cups flour
1 tablespoon melted butter

Previous page:
The kitchen garden is planted between the Heikki and Maria Ketola House and a small apple orchard at Old World Wisconsin.
GERALD H. EMMERICH JR.

In a large bowl, stir yeast and sugar into warm water; let stand 5 minutes to soften. Stir in salt and shortening. Add rye meal; beat until smooth. Adding 1 cup at a time, beat in enough flour to make a stiff dough. Turn out onto a lightly floured board. Cover with a dry cloth; let stand 5 to 15 minutes. Wash and grease bowl; set aside. Grease a large baking sheet; set aside. Adding flour as necessary to prevent sticking, knead dough until smooth, about 10 minutes. Place in greased bowl, turning all sides. Cover and let rise in a warm place until doubled in bulk, about 2 hours. Punch down dough; shape into a ball. Flatten to a round loaf, 10 inches in diameter. Pressing with your fingers and thumbs, make a hole in center. Stretch until hole is 2 inches in diameter. Place shaped loaf on prepared baking sheet. Cover and let dough rise until doubled in bulk, about 1 hour. Use tines of a fork to make punctures over top of loaf. Bake 30 to 35 minutes or until golden brown. Brush top of hot loaf with melted butter. Cool on rack.[2]

Vegetable Soup

This soup is simple, delicious, and straight from the garden.

new potatoes
vegetables (carrots, peas, beans, rutabagas, etc.)
2 tablespoons butter
2 tablespoons flour
1 cup milk
1 egg yolk
¼ to ½ cup cream
salt and pepper, to taste

Use new potatoes and whatever fresh vegetables are ready, such as carrots, peas, beans, rutabagas, etc. Chop all vegetables small. Mix in pot and cover with water. Bring to a boil and simmer until vegetables are tender. Separate stock and vegetables.

Melt butter. Add flour and blend with fork. Pour into hot vegetable stock. Beat and add milk. Combine egg yolk and cream and add slowly to stock. Add vegetables, salt, and pepper.[3]

Vegetables and meat are cooked together in one pot for a simple meal.
SANDRA MATSON

Mojakka

Whether prepared as a soup or a stew, *mojakka* was served frequently in Finnish households. Any available meat or vegetables may be used for this one-pot meal.

2 pounds venison or beef cut in large cubes
2 tablespoons butter
4 carrots, cut into large pieces
4 to 5 potatoes, cut into large pieces
salt and pepper

Brown meat in butter in a frying pan. Combine meat and vegetables in deep baking dish. Cover half way with water. Add salt and pepper. Bake at least 1 hour or until meat breaks with a fork. For stew: prepare on stove, and add a little flour to thicken gravy.[4]

Rutabaga Casserole *(Länttulaatikko)*

Ah, the Finns and their rutabagas! Rutabagas were grown in the kitchen garden for the family in addition to being grown in the field to feed the cows. This casserole is a Finnish kitchen classic. Turnips may also be used.

2½ pounds rutabagas/turnips, peeled and cut into small squares (2 cups vegetables)
¼ cup bread crumbs (*pulla* bread crumbs, if available)
¼ cup heavy cream
½ teaspoon nutmeg
3 teaspoons salt
2 eggs, lightly beaten
2 tablespoons plus 2 teaspoons soft butter
2 tablespoons hard butter, cut into tiny bits

Heat stove. Boil rutabagas/turnips in water on stove top until tender. Drain and sieve or puree rutabagas/turnips. Soak the bread crumbs in heavy cream for a few minutes; stir in nutmeg, salt, and eggs. Add pureed rutabagas and mix thoroughly. Stir in 2 tablespoons soft butter. Grease casserole dish with remaining soft butter; put rutabaga mixture into casserole. Dot with hard butter bits and bake uncovered for 1 hour or until top is lightly browned.[5]

Pulla

***Pulla* is a moist, rich, sweet bread flavored with cardamom. It's delicious hot or cool and well worth making.**

1 cup milk
½ cup sugar
½ teaspoon salt
1 teaspoon cardamom
2 eggs, beaten
4 to 6 cups flour, divided
1¼ teaspoons yeast
¼ cup warm water
¼ cup melted butter
1 egg, beaten

Scald milk and let cool. Combine milk, sugar, salt, cardamom, eggs, and 1 cup flour to make a smooth batter. Dissolve yeast in warm water. Add yeast to batter and stir. Stir in butter. Add flour until dough pulls away. Let rest on floured board for 15 minutes. Knead until elastic.

Put in greased bowl; let rise until double (1 hour). Punch down dough and put on floured board. Cut into three strips, braid, and turn ends under. Put in greased pan and let rise 30 to 40 minutes. Cover with beaten egg. Bake 30 minutes.[6]

Finnish Rice Pudding *(Riisipuuro)*

Following the day's main meal the Finns traditionally served a light and refreshing dessert such as pudding, porridge, or fruit soup. Rice pudding was a classic choice.

¾ cup rice, uncooked
¾ cup water
2 tablespoons butter
4 cups milk
1 teaspoon salt
1 3-inch cinnamon stick
¼ teaspoon nutmeg
1 teaspoon vanilla
1 tablespoon cinnamon
½ cup sugar
¼ cup melted butter

In large saucepan, combine rice and water. Bring to a boil and stir in butter, milk, salt, and cinnamon stick. Cover and simmer over low heat about an hour. You can use a double boiler instead of a saucepan to avoid any scorching problem; then increase the cooking time by at least half an hour. When pudding is thick, remove cinnamon stick and stir in nutmeg and vanilla. Mix the cinnamon and sugar together and serve over the hot pudding with melted butter.[7]

ON THE JOURNEY.

VICK'S ILLUSTRATED MONTHLY MAGAZINE 6, 1883

Appendix: Plant Tables

PLANTS COMMONLY GROWN FOR THE TABLE BY YANKEES IN WISCONSIN

Category	Common Name	Botanical Latin
Root Vegetables	Beet	*Beta vulgaris* var. *crassa*
	Carrot	*Daucus carota*
	Parsnip	*Pastinaca sativa*
	Potato	*Solanum tuberosum*
	Salsify	*Tragopogon porrifolius*
	Turnip	*Brassica rapa*
Coles	Cabbage	*Brassica oleracea* var. *capitata*
Alliums	Onion	*Allium cepa* var. *cepa*
Greens	Lettuce	*Lactuca sativa*
	Spinach	*Spinacia oleracea*
Legumes	Bean, Bush	*Phaseolus vulgaris*
	Bean, Pole	*Phaseolus vulgaris*
	Pea	*Pisum sativum*
Etc.	Pepper	*Capsium annuum*
	Squash, Cushaw	*Cucurbita mixta*
	Squash, Summer	*Cucurbita pepo*
	Squash, Winter (Hubbard)	*Cucurbita maxima*
	Tomato	*Solanum lycopersicum*
Herbs	Parsley	*Petroselinum crispum*
	Sage	*Salvia officinalis*
	Sweet Marjoram	*Origanum majorana*
	Thyme	*Thymus vulgaris*

PLANTS COMMONLY GROWN FOR THE TABLE BY GERMANS IN WISCONSIN

Category	Common Name	Botanical Latin
Root Vegetables	Beet	*Beta vulgaris* var. *crassa*
	Carrot	*Daucus carota*
	Celeriac	*Apium graveolens* var. *rapaceum*
	Horseradish	*Armoracia rusticana*
	Potato	*Solanum tuberosum*
	Radish, Summer	*Raphanus sativus*
	Radish, Winter	*Raphanus sativus*
	Root Parsley	*Petroselinum crispum tuberosum*
	Scorzonera	*Scorzonera hispanica*
	Turnip	*Brassica rapa*
Coles	Cabbage, Green	*Brassica oleracea* var. *capitata*
	Cabbage, Red	*Brassica oleracea* var. *capitata*
	Cabbage, Savoy	*Brassica oleracea* var. *sabauda*
	Kale	*Brassica oleracea* var. *acephala*
	Kohlrabi	*Brassica oleracea* var. *gongylodes*
Alliums	Garlic	*Allium sativum*
	Leek	*Allium porrum*
	Onion	*Allium cepa* var. *cepa*
Greens	Corn Salad	*Valerianella locusta*
	Endive	*Chicorium endivia*
	Lettuce	*Lactuca sativa*
	Spinach	*Spinacia oleracea*
Legumes	Bean, Bush	*Phaseolus vulgaris*
	Bean, Runner	*Phaseolus coccineus*
	Pea	*Pisum sativum*
Etc.	Cucumber	*Cucumis sativus*
Herbs	Caraway	*Carum carvi*
	Dill	*Anethum graveolens*
	Parsley	*Petroselinum crispum*
	Summer Savory	*Satureja hortensis*
	Sweet Marjoram	*Origanum majorana*
	Thyme	*Thymus vulgaris*

PLANTS COMMONLY GROWN FOR THE TABLE BY NORWEGIANS IN WISCONSIN

Category	Common Name	Botanical Latin
Root Vegetables	Beet	*Beta vulgaris* var. *crassa*
	Carrot	*Daucus carota*
	Potato	*Solanum tuberosum*
	Rutabaga	*Brassica napus*
	Turnip	*Brassica rapa*
Coles	Cabbage	*Brassica oleracea* var. *capitata*
Alliums	Onion	*Allium cepa* var. *cepa*
Etc.	Cucumber	*Cucumis sativus*
	Watermelon	*Citrullus lanatus*
Herbs	Caraway	*Carum carvi*
	Dill	*Anethum graveolens*
	Mint	*Mentha* spp.
	Parsley	*Petroselinum crispum*
	Sweet Marjoram	*Origanum majorana*
	Thyme	*Thymus vulgaris*

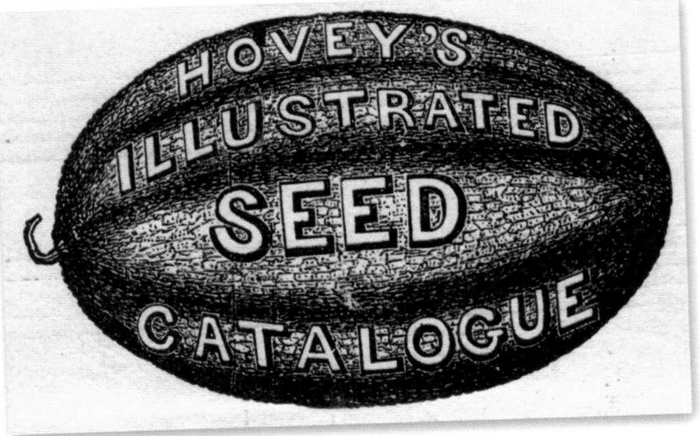

LEFT: *THE LADIES' FLORAL CABINET AND PICTORIAL HOME COMPANION* 5, MARCH 1876

RIGHT: *THE LADIES' FLORAL CABINET AND PICTORIAL HOME COMPANION* 4, JANUARY 1875

PLANTS COMMONLY GROWN FOR THE TABLE BY IRISH IN WISCONSIN

Category	Common Name	Botanical Latin
Root Vegetables	Potato	*Solanum tuberosum*
	Rutabaga	*Brassica napus*
	Turnip	*Brassica rapa*
Coles	Cabbage	*Brassica oleracea* var. *capitata*
Alliums	Leek	*Allium porrum*
	Onion	*Allium cepa* var. *cepa*
Herbs	Parsley	*Petroselinum crispum*

PLANTS COMMONLY GROWN FOR THE TABLE BY DANES IN WISCONSIN

Category	Common Name	Botanical Latin
Root Vegetables	Beet	*Beta vulgaris* var. *crassa*
	Carrot	*Daucus carota*
	Parsnip	*Pastinaca sativa*
	Potato	*Solanum tuberosum*
	Radish	*Raphanus sativus*
	Turnip	*Brassica rapa*
Coles	Cabbage, Green	*Brassica oleracea* var. *capitata*
	Cabbage, Red	*Brassica oleracea* var. *capitata*
	Kale	*Brassica oleracea* var. *acephala*
Alliums	Onion	*Allium cepa* var. *cepa*
Legumes	Bean, Navy	*Phaseolus vulgaris*
	Pea	*Pisum sativum*
Etc.	Celery	*Apium graveolens* var. *dulce*
	Cucumber	*Cucumis sativus*
Herbs	Caraway	*Carum carvi*
	Chives	*Allium schoenoprasum*
	Dill	*Anethum graveolens*
	Parsley	*Petroselinum crispum*

PLANTS COMMONLY GROWN FOR THE TABLE BY POLES IN WISCONSIN

Category	Common Name	Botanical Latin
Root Vegetables	Beet	*Beta vulgaris* var. *crassa*
	Carrot	*Daucus carota*
	Celeriac	*Apium graveolens* var. *rapaceum*
	Horseradish	*Armoracia rusticana*
	Parsnip	*Pastinaca sativa*
	Potato	*Solanum tuberosum*
	Root Parsley	*Petroselinum crispum tuberosum*
	Rutabaga	*Brassica napus*
	Turnip	*Brassica rapa*
Coles	Cabbage	*Brassica oleracea* var. *capitata*
	Kohlrabi	*Brassica oleracea* var. *gongylodes*
Alliums	Onion	*Allium cepa* var. *cepa*
Greens	Lettuce	*Lactuca sativa*
Legumes	Bean, Bush	*Phaseolus vulgaris*
	Beans, Pole	*Phaseolus vulgaris*
	Beans, Runner	*Phaseolus coccineus*
	Pea	*Pisum sativum*
Etc.	Cucumber	*Cucumis sativus*
Herbs	Caraway	*Carum carvi*
	Chives	*Allium schoenoprasum*
	Dill	*Anethum graveolens*
	Parsley	*Petroselinum crispum*
	Poppy	*Papaver*
	Sage	*Salvia officinalis*
	Sweet Marjoram	*Origanum majorana*
	Thyme	*Thymus vulgaris*

PLANTS COMMONLY GROWN FOR THE TABLE BY FINNS IN WISCONSIN

Category	Common Name	Botanical Latin
Root Vegetables	Beet	*Beta vulgaris* var. *crassa*
	Carrot	*Daucus carota*
	Potato	*Solanum tuberosum*
	Rutabaga	*Brassica napus*
	Turnip	*Brassica rapa*
Coles	Cabbage	*Brassica oleracea* var. *capitata*
Alliums	Onion	*Allium cepa* var. *cepa*
Legumes	Bean, Bush	*Phaseolus vulgaris*
	Pea	*Pisum sativum*
Etc.	Cucumber	*Cucumis sativus*
Herbs	Caraway	*Carum carvi*
	Dill	*Anethum graveolens*
	Parsley	*Petroselinum crispum*
	Thyme	*Thymus vulgaris*

LEFT: *THE LADIES' FLORAL CABINET AND PICTORIAL HOME COMPANION* 4, JULY 1875

RIGHT: *THE LADIES' FLORAL CABINET AND PICTORIAL HOME COMPANION* 4, JANUARY 1875

Notes

INTRODUCTION

1. Martin C. Perkins, personal correspondence, April 2010.

2. Arthur R. Boerner, "How Roses Came to Wisconsin Frontiers, an Account: Historic Roses of Wisconsin," 1948, cited in William J. Radler, personal correspondence, April 8, 2008.

CHAPTER 1

1. Edgar Sanders, "The Kitchen Garden," *The Illustrated Annual Register of Rural Affairs for 1858*, no. 4. (Albany, NY: Luther Tucker & Son, 1858), 84.

2. Ibid., 84.

3. Fearing Burr Jr., *The Field and Garden Vegetables of America* (Boston: Crosby and Nichols, 1863), 389.

4. Jacob Conrad, "The James Harvey Sanford House: A Yankee Home and Farm of Walworth County Wisconsin, ca. 1860" (Old World Wisconsin unpublished manuscript, March 31, 2005), 24.

5. *Vick's Flower and Vegetable Garden* (Rochester, NY: James Vick, 1880), 184.

6. F. K. Phoenix, "Horticulture: Nurseries in the North-West—should they not be sustained?" *Wisconsin & Iowa Farmer, and Northwestern Cultivator*, vol. 3 (Racine, WI: Mark Miller, 1851), 60.

7. A. J. Downing, "The National Ignorance of the Agricultural Interest," written for *The Horticulturist*, September 1851, republished in *Rural Essays* (New York: R. Worthington, 1881), 391–392.

8. *Wisconsin & Iowa Farmer, and Northwestern Cultivator*, vol. 6 (Janesville, WI: Mark Miller and S. P. Lathrop, March 1854), 49.

9. Henry Ward Beecher, *Plain and Pleasant Talk About Fruits, Flowers and Farming* (New York: Derby & Jackson, 1859), 199.

10. John F. Hauser, "The Vegetable Garden," *Wisconsin Farmers' Institutes: A Hand-Book of Agriculture*, no. 10. (Milwaukee: Wisconsin Farmers' Institutes, 1896), 78.

CHAPTER 2

1. Allen F. Johnson, "The Wesley P. Benson House: A Vermont-Yankee Craftsman's Household in the Village of Fort Atkinson, Jefferson County, Wisconsin" (Old World Wisconsin unpublished manuscript, August 13, 1982), 59–63.

2. The price for Excelsior Hand Lawn Mowers. *B. K. Bliss and Son's Illustrated Spring Catalogue and Amateurs Guide to the Flower and Kitchen Garden* (New York: B. K. Bliss & Son, 1872), 109.

3. Ibid., 111–113.

4. *Vick's Flower and Vegetable Garden* (Rochester, NY: James Vick, 1876), 11.

5. Ibid., 18.

6. Mrs. S. O. Johnson, *Every Woman Her Own Flower Gardener* (New York: Henry T. Williams, 1875), 62.

7. *D. M. Ferry & Co.'s Catalogue of Garden, Flower and Agricultural Seeds* (Detroit: O. S. Gulley's Stram Presses, 1876), 103.

8. Johnson, *Every Woman Her Own Flower Gardener*, 5.

9. Ibid., 6.

10. Johnson, "The Wesley P. Benson House," 13–16.

11. Ibid., 31.

YANKEE RECIPES

1. Sarah Josepha Hale, *Early American Cookery: "The Good Housekeeper," 1841* (Mineola, NY: Dover Publication Inc., 1996), 27–28.

2. *Wisconsin & Iowa Farmer, and Northwestern Cultivator*, vol. 7 (Janesville, WI: Mark Miller and S. P. Lathrop, 1855), 344. Old World Wisconsin Master Recipe File (James and Rebecca Sanford Farm section).

3. Ibid., 147.

4. *Godey's Lady's Book and Magazine*, vol. 90 (Philadelphia: Louis A. Godey, 1875), 375. Old World Wisconsin Master Recipe File (James and Rebecca Sanford Farm section).

5. *Wisconsin & Iowa Farmer*, 84.

6. Ibid., 85.

7. Ibid., 117.

8. Mary Randolph, *The Virginia Housewife* (Washington, DC: Davis and Force, 1824), 168. Old World Wisconsin Master Recipe File (Wesley and Sophia Benson House section).

9. Compiled by Ladies of Toronto and Chief Cities and Towns in Canada, *The Home Cook Book* (Toronto, Canada: The Musson Book Co. Ltd., 1877), 171. Old World Wisconsin Master Recipe File (Wesley and Sophia Benson House section).

10. *Wisconsin & Iowa Farmer, and Northwestern Cultivator*, vol. 5 (Janesville, WI: Mark Miller, 1853), 67.

11. *Vick's Flower and Vegetable Garden* (Rochester, NY: James Vick, 1876), 111.

12. E. Hutchinson, *Ladies' Indispensable Assistant* (New York: F. J. Dow & Co., 1852), 35; Old World Wisconsin Master Recipe File (James and Rebecca Sanford Farm section).

CHAPTER 3

1. James William Miller, "German Heirloom Gardening Research Report" (Old World Wisconsin unpublished manuscript, February 2002), 9.

2. Ibid., 13–14.

3. Ibid., 115–122.

4. "Der Garten als Hausapotheke," *Acker- und Gartenbau-Zeitung* (January 1, 1890), 12, cited by James William Miller, "German Heirloom Gardening Research Report" (Old World Wisconsin unpublished manuscript, February 2002), 126.

5. "Der Garten als Hausapotheke," *Acker- und Gartenbau-Zeitung* (September 15, 1889), 334–335, cited by James William Miller, "German Heirloom Gardening Research Report" (Old World Wisconsin unpublished manuscript, February 2002), 125.

6. Korinne Oberle, "Schulz Farm Interpretive Plan" (Old World Wisconsin unpublished manuscript, 1977), 30.

7. Mark Knipping, "A Pomeranian Wheat Farm of Dodge County, Wisconsin (ca. 1860)" (Old World Wisconsin unpublished manuscript, February 1, 1977), 95.

CHAPTER 4

1. *The History of Washington and Ozaukee Counties, Wisconsin* (Chicago: Western Historical Company, 1881), 524–525.

2. Martin C. Perkins, "The Friedrich Koepsell Farm: A Pomeranian Carpenter's Farmstead of Washington County (ca. 1880)" (Old World Wisconsin unpublished manuscript, August 31, 1978), 60–61.

GERMAN RECIPES

1. Henriette Davidis, *Praktisches Kochbuch für die Deutschen in Amerika*, 2nd ed. (Milwaukee, WI: Brumder, 1897), 43, in James William Miller, "German Heirloom Gardening Research Report" (Old World Wisconsin unpublished manuscript, February 2002), 131.

2. *Black kitchen* refers to an architectural carryover from the Old Country in which one enclosed interior room combines the functions of cooking, smoking, and heating. The Charles and Auguste Schulz House includes one of these rare black kitchens.

3. Old World Wisconsin Master Recipe File (Charles and Auguste Schulz Farm section).

4. Old World Wisconsin Master Recipe File (Friedrich and Sophia Koepsell Farm section).

5. Old World Wisconsin Master Recipe File (Friedrich and Sophia Koepsell Farm section).

6. Henriette Löffler, Großes *Illustriertes Kochbuch für einfachen Tisch und die feine Küche*, 10th ed. (Stuttgart: J. Ebner, 1882), fascimile ed. (Dreieich: KG Buchproduktion, 2000), 215, in James William Miller, "German Heirloom Gardening Research Report" (Old World Wisconsin unpublished manuscript, February 2002), 137.

7. Frieda Ritzerow, *Mecklenburgisches Kochbuch* (Rostock: Hinstorff Verlagsbuchandlucng, 1868), facsimile ed. (Rostock: Hinstorff Verlag, 1981), 192, in James William Miller, "German Heirloom Gardening Research Report" (Old World Wisconsin unpublished manuscript, February 2002), 141.

8. *The Ethnic Epicure* (Wauwatosa, WI: Wauwatosa Junior Woman's Club, 1973), 59. Old World Wisconsin Master Recipe File (Friedrich and Sophia Koepsell Farm section).

9. Ibid., 66. Old World Wisconsin Master Recipe File (Charles and Auguste Schulz Farm section).

10. Ritzerow, *Mecklenburgisches Kochbuch*, 113, in James William Miller, "German Heirloom Gardening Research Report" (Old World Wisconsin unpublished manuscript, February 2002), 134.

11. Henriette Davidis, *Zuverlässige und selbstgeprüfte Recepte der gewöhliche und feineren Küche* (Osnabrück: Rackhorst'schen Buchhandlung, 1845), facsimile ed. (Wetter: Evangelische Kirchengemeinde Vorlmarstein-Oberwengern, 1994), 96, in James William Miller, "German Heirloom Gardening Research Report" (Old World Wisconsin unpublished manuscript, February 2002), 143.

CHAPTER 5

1. Richard J. Fapso, *Norwegians in Wisconsin* (Madison: Wisconsin Historical Society Press, 2001), 8.

2. Hjalmar R. Holand, *Coon Valley: An Historical Account of the Norwegian Congregation in Coon County* (Minneapolis: 1928, English translation La Crosse, WI: Litho-Graphics, 1976), 37, cited in Mark H. Knipping and Richard J. Fapso, "The Anders Ellingsen Kvaale Farm: Early Norwegian Commercial Agriculture, circa 1865" (Old World Wisconsin unpublished manuscript, January 16, 1978), 16.

3. L. M. Bothum, *En Historie fra Nybyggerlivet* (Dalton, MN: L. M. Bothum, 1915), 104–105, quoted in Jon Gjerde, *From Peasants to Farmers* (Cambridge: Cambridge University Press, 1985), 194.

4. Not all newcomers appreciated unfamiliar produce. A Norwegian woman recalling life farther west in the Dakota Territory in 1880 wrote: "Each homesteader received from the government free packages of garden seeds. The seeds were planted in the newly broken soil but the newcomers did not know what would come up and, in many instances, did not know what to do with the vegetables since they were not familiar with them. Huge watermelons grew on the fertile land but the women tried without success to cook them in various ways and ended up by feeding them to the cattle." "Nellie Proper Beachem Hunstead. Brown County. 1880," *Daughters of Dakota: Schooled in Privation*, 4 (Yankton, SD: General Federation of Women's Clubs of South Dakota/Daughters of Dakota, 1991), 65.

5. Halvor L. Skavlem, *The Skavlem and Odegaarden Families* (Madison, WI: Tracy & Kilagore Printers, 1915), 111, cited in Mark H. Knipping and Richard J. Fapso, "The Anders Ellingsen Kvaale Farm: Early Norwegian Commercial Agriculture, circa 1865" (Old World Wisconsin unpublished manuscript, January 16, 1978), 82.

6. Elisabeth Koren, *The Diary of Elisabeth Koren, 1853–1855*, trans. and ed. David T. Nelson (Northfield, MN: Norwegian-American Historical Association, 1955), 294.

7. Linka Preus, *Linka's Diary on Land and Sea, 1845–1864*, trans. and ed. Johan C. K. Preus and Diderikke Brandt Preus (Minneapolis: Augsburg Publishing House, 1952), 213, quoted in Doris Weatherford, *Foreign and Female: Immigrant Women in America, 1840–1930* (New York: Facts on File Inc., 1995), 155.

8. Richard J. Fapso and Mark H. Knipping, "The Knud Crispinusen Fossebrekke House: A Norwegian Settler's Cabin in the Woods, ca. 1845" (Old World Wisconsin unpublished manuscript, June 30, 1978), 59.

9. Ibid., 63.

10. Nels Crispensen, interview, August 1939, cited in Ibid., 59.

11. Ibid., 66.

12. Mark H. Knipping and Richard J. Fapso, "The Anders Ellingsen Kvaale Farm: Early Norwegian Commercial Agriculture, circa 1865" (Old World Wisconsin unpublished manuscript, January 16, 1978), 45–50, 69.

13. Ibid., 71–77.

14. Ibid., 63.

15. Doris Weatherford, *Foreign and Female: Immigrant Women in America, 1840–1930* (New York: Facts on File Inc., 1995), 157.

NORWEGIAN RECIPES

1. Old World Wisconsin Master Recipe File (Anders and Christina Kvaale Farm section).

2. Probably *Mentha canadensis* (*M. arvensis*).

3. Old World Wisconsin Master Recipe File (Knud and Gertrude Fossebrekke Farm section).

4. Ibid.

5. Ibid.

6. Ibid.

7. Old World Wisconsin Master Recipe File (Anders and Christina Kvaale Farm section).

8. Compiled by the Volunteers of the Norwegian-American Museum, *Pioneer Cookbook* (Decorah, IA: Vesterheim Norwegian-American Museum, 1969), 48. Old World Wisconsin Master Recipe File (Anders and Christina Kvaale Farm section).

9. Old World Wisconsin Master Recipe File (Anders and Christina Kvaale Farm section).

10. Ibid.

11. Ibid.

12. Volunteers of the Norwegian-American Museum, *Pioneer Cookbook*, 170. Old World Wisconsin Master Recipe File (Anders and Christina Kvaale Farm section).

CHAPTER 6

1. David G. Holmes, *Irish in Wisconsin* (Madison: Wisconsin Historical Society Press, 2004), 14.

2. Ibid., 16.

3. Terence Reeves-Smyth, *The Garden Lover's Guide to Ireland* (New York: Princeton Architectural Press, 2001), 9, 47.

4. E. Estyn Evans, *Irish Folk Ways* (New York: The Devin-Adair Company, 1957), 20.

5. Allen F. Johnson, "The Mary Hafford House: An Irish Widow's Household in the Village of Hubbleton, Jefferson County, Wisconsin" (Old World Wisconsin unpublished manuscript, January 20, 1982), 28.

6. I. Weld, *Roscommon: Statistical Survey of the County of Roscommon* (Dublin: R. Graisberry, Printer to the Royal Dublin Society, 1832), cited in E. Estyn Evans, *Irish Folk Ways* (New York: The Devin-Adair Company, 1957), 83.

7. Evans, *Irish Folk Ways*, 83.

8. Ibid., 10.

9. Ibid., 11.

10. Margaret M. Mulrooney, *Black Powder, White Lace: The du Pont Irish and Cultural Identity in Nineteenth-Century America* (Hanover, NH, and London: University Press of New England, 2002), 165–173, 185.

11. Johnson, "The Mary Hafford House," 2–5.

12. Ibid., 2.

13. Ibid., 10.

IRISH RECIPES

1. Miller family, County Roscommon, circa 1857. Old World Wisconsin Master Recipe File (Mary Hafford House section).

2. Mrs. Ethel Finnel, Hubbleton, Wisconsin. Old World Wisconsin Master Recipe File (Mary Hafford House section).

3. Old World Wisconsin Master Recipe File (Mary Hafford House section).

4. Harva Hachten and Terese Allen, *The Flavor of Wisconsin* (Madison: Wisconsin Historical Society Press, 2009), 180–181.

5. Old World Wisconsin Master Recipe File (Mary Hafford House section).

6. *Home Cook Book* (Toledo, OH: T. J. Brown, Eager & Co., 1876), 216. Old World Wisconsin Master Recipe File (Mary Hafford House section).

7. Harva Hachten, *The Flavor of Wisconsin* (Madison: The State Historical Society of Wisconsin, 1986), 316; Old World Wisconsin Master Recipe File (Mary Hafford House section).

8. Patrick Logan, *Irish Country Cures* (New York: Sterling Publishing Co. Inc., 1994), 44.

9. *Mrs. Owens' Cookbook* (Chicago: J. B. Smiley, 1881), 320. Old World Wisconsin Master Recipe File (Mary Hafford House section).

CHAPTER 7

1. Frederick Hale, *Danes in Wisconsin* (Madison: Wisconsin Historical Society Press, 2005), 18.

2. Ellen Johansen Pedersen, "As I Remember . . ." (typewritten copy in Old World Wisconsin files, ca. 1975).

3. Rolf Toman, ed., *European Garden Design from Classical Antiquity to the Present Day* (Bonn, Germany: Tandem Verlag GmbH, 2007), 342.

4. Karl-Dietrich Bühler, *The Scandinavian Garden* (London: Frances Lincoln Limited, 2000), 6.

5. Toman, *European Garden Design*, 342.

6. Bühler, *The Scandinavian Garden*, 6.

7. Mark H. Knipping, "The Kristen Pedersen Farm: A Danish Dairy Farm of Polk County, Wisconsin, circa 1890" (Old World Wisconsin unpublished manuscript, September 26, 1980), 36.

8. T. W. Gibbs, "For Sale: 40,000 Acres of Select Farming Land Known as the 'Cushing' Lands, in Polk County, Wisconsin," from "Choice Farming Land in the St. Croix Valley, Polk County, Wisconsin: For Sale to Settlers by Caleb Cushing" (Madison, WI: Atwater & Culver, 1875), cited in Mark H. Knipping, "The Kristen Pedersen Farm: A Danish Dairy Farm of Polk County, Wisconsin, circa 1890" (Old World Wisconsin unpublished manuscript, September 26, 1980), 91.

9. Knipping, "The Kristen Pedersen Farm," 75.

10. Bühler, *The Scandinavian Garden*, 176, 178.

11. Knipping, "The Kristen Pedersen Farm," 121–122.

12. E. J. Perry, *Among the Danish Farmers* (Danville, IL: The Interstate, 1939), cited in Ibid., 17.

13. Ibid., 17.

14. Knipping, "The Kristen Pedersen Farm," 122.

15. Perry, *Among the Danish Farmers*, 17.

16. Knipping, "The Kristen Pedersen Farm," 116.

17. Ibid., 107–114.

18. Ibid., 117–118.

19. Ibid., 119.

20. Ibid., 125.

21. Ibid., 137–138.

DANISH RECIPES

1. *The Cooking of Scandinavia: Recipe Booklet* (Alexandria, VA: Time-Life Books, 1968), 48.

2. Old World Wisconsin Master Recipe File (Kristen Pedersen Farm section).

3. Beatrice Ojakangas, *Scandinavian Cooking* (Tucson, AZ: HP Books, 1983), 135.

4. Old World Wisconsin Master Recipe File (Kristen Pedersen Farm section).

5. Ibid.

6. Credited to Katrine Paulsen, Old World Wisconsin Master Recipe File (Kristen Pedersen Farm section).

7. *The Cooking of Scandinavia: Recipe Booklet*, 54.

8. *The Ethnic Epicure: A Treasury of Old World Wisconsin Recipes* (Wauwatosa, WI: Wauwatosa Junior Woman's Club, 1973), 119.

9. Nika Standen Hazelton, *The Art of Danish Cooking* (New York: Doubleday & Co. Inc., 1964), 159.

10. Ojakangas, *Scandinavian Cooking*, 22.

CHAPTER 8

1. Michael J. Goc, *Native Realm, The Polish-American Community of Portage County 1857–1992* (Stevens Point and Friendship, WI: Worzalla Publishing and New Past Press Inc., 1992), 22.

2. Ibid., 18–19.

3. Susan G. Mikos, "Folkways of Polish Immigrants" (Old World Wisconsin unpublished manuscript, March 22, 1999), 1.

4. Ibid., 2.

5. Goc, *Native Realm*, 22.

6. Mikos, "Folkways of Polish Immigrants," 17.

7. Goc, *Native Realm*, 34, 37.

8. Maria Dembińska, *Food and Drink in Medieval Poland*, trans. Magdelena Thomas, revised and adapted William Woys Weaver (Philadelphia: University of Pennsylvania Press, 1999), 130.

9. Mikos, "Folkways of Polish Immigrants," 31.

10. Kathleen A. Ernst, "Kruza House Interpretive Plan" (Old World Wisconsin unpublished manuscript, 1989), 9, 10.

11. Mikos, "Folkways of Polish Immigrants," 27.

12. Ibid., Appendix 1: "Shawano County Lifetime Support Agreements."

13. Dr. Danuta Mazurek, quoted in Susan Davis Price, *Growing Home: Stories of Ethnic Gardening* (Minneapolis: University of Minnesota Press, 2000), 147.

POLISH RECIPES

1. *Kasha* refers to any porridge cereal (buckwheat, wheat, oats, rye, and, in this recipe, barley).

2. Maria Lemnis and Henryk Vitry, *Old Polish Traditions in the Kitchen and at the Table*, trans. Eliza Lewandowska (Warsaw, Poland: Interpress Publishers, 1981), 32–33.

3. Ibid., 262.

4. Harva Hachten and Terese Allen, *The Flavor of Wisconsin* (Madison: Wisconsin Historical Society Press, 2009), 259.

5. Lemnis and Vitry, *Old Polish Traditions*, 277.

6. Hachten and Allen, *The Flavor of Wisconsin*, 276.

7. Lemnis and Vitry, *Old Polish Traditions*, 195–199.

CHAPTER 9

1. John I. Kolehmainen, *The Finns in America: A Students' Guide to Localized History* (New York: New York Teachers College Press, 1968), 11, quoted in Mark H. Knipping, Richard H. Zeitlin, and Peter D. Frank, "The Jacob Rankinen Farm: A Finnish Homestead in the Cutover, circa 1897" (Old World Wisconsin unpublished manuscript, March 24, 1978), 13.

2. Mark H. Knipping, Richard H. Zeitlin, and Peter D. Frank, "The Jacob Rankinen Farm: A Finnish Homestead in the Cutover, circa 1897" (Old World Wisconsin unpublished manuscript, March 24, 1978), 52, and family interviews, Old World Wisconsin files, "Jacob Rankinen Farm," 1976.

3. Mark H. Knipping, *Finns in Wisconsin* (Madison: Wisconsin Historical Society Press, 2008), 29.

4. Kristiina Niemistö, *From Köyhäjoki Kaustinen to Florida*, trans. Maija Salo Cravens, quoted in Mark Knipping, *Finns in Wisconsin* (Madison: Wisconsin Historical Society Press, 2008), 59.

5. Ibid., 58.

6. Knipping, Zeitlin, and Frank, "The Jacob Rankinen Farm," 53, 54.

7. Ibid., 65–67.

8. Ibid., 64.

9. Ibid., 68.

10. Mark H. Knipping and Richard H. Zeitlin, "The Heikki Ketola Farm: A Finnish Dairy Farm in Bayfield County, circa 1915" (Old World Wisconsin unpublished manuscript, April 15, 1978), 19–20.

11. Ibid., 20.

12. *Wisconsin Farmers' Institutes: A Hand-Book of Agriculture*, no. 17. (Madison: Wisconsin Farmers' Institutes, 1903), 227.

13. Knipping and Zeitlin, "The Heikki Ketola Farm," 29–31.

14. Ibid., 15.

15. Ibid., 24.

16. Ibid.

17. Knipping, Zeitlin, and Frank, "The Jacob Rankinen Farm," 55–56.

FINNISH RECIPES

1. Nika Standen Hazelton, *The Art of Scandinavian Cooking* (New York: Macmillan Company, 1965), 143.

2. Beatrice Ojakangas, *Scandinavian Cooking* (Tucson, AZ: HP Books, 1983), 134.

3. Old World Wisconsin Master Recipe File (Heikki and Maria Ketola Farm section).

4. Old World Wisconsin Master Recipe File (Jacob and Louisa Rankinen Farm section).

5. Old World Wisconsin Master Recipe File (Heikki and Maria Ketola Farm section).

6. Ibid.

7. Carolyn Larson, ed., *Taste of Tradition: Old World Wisconsin Cooking* (Eagle, WI: The Friends of Old World Wisconsin, 1988), 154.

Stone-edged flower beds and potted plants on the windowsill brighten the Nels Wickstrom family home in Florence County, 1891.

WHI IMAGE ID 3187

Selected Bibliography

YANKEES

Adams, Denise Wiles. *Restoring American Gardens: An Encyclopedia of Heirloom Ornamental Plants, 1640–1940*. Portland, OR: Timber Press, 2004.

Bailey, L. H. *Cyclopedia of American Horticulture*. 4 vols. New York: The MacMillan Company, 1901, 1902, 1903.

Becker, Robert F. "Vegetable Gardening in the United States: A History, 1565–1900." *HortScience* 19, no. 5 (October 1984).

Beecher, Henry Ward. *Plain and Pleasant Talk About Fruit, Flowers and Farming*. New York: Derby & Jackson, 1859.

Bennet, Ida D. *The Flower Garden*. New York: McClure, Phillips & Co, 1903.

B. K. Bliss and Son's Illustrated Spring Catalogue and Amateurs Guide to the Flower and Kitchen Garden. New York: B. K. Bliss & Son, 1872.

Breck, Joseph. *New Book of Flowers*. New York: Orange Judd & Company, 1866.

Bridgeman, Thomas. *The Young Gardener's Assistant*. New York: published by the author, 1853.

Buist, Robert. *American Flower-Garden Directory*. New York: Orange Judd & Company, 1854.

Buist, Robert. *The Family Kitchen Gardener*. New York: A. O. Moore, Agricultural Book Publisher, 1858.

Burr, Fearing, Jr. *The Field and Garden Vegetables of America*. Boston: Crosby and Nichols, 1863.

Burr, Fearing, Jr. *The Field and Garden Vegetables of America*. Chillicothe, IL: The American Botanist, Booksellers, 1988. Reprint of second edition, Boston, 1865.

Conrad, Jacob. "The James Harvey Sanford House: A Yankee Home and Farm of Walworth County, Wisconsin, ca. 1860." Old World Wisconsin unpublished manuscript, March 31, 2005.

D. M. Ferry & Co.'s Catalogue of Garden, Flower and Agricultural Seeds. Detroit: O. S. Culley's Stram Presses, 1876.

Downing, A. J. *Rural Essays*. New York: R. Worthington, 1881.

The Gardener's Manual. New York: The United Society, 1843.

Hachten, Harva. *The Flavor of Wisconsin*. Madison: The State Historical Society of Wisconsin, 1986.

Hachten, Harva, and Terese Allen. *The Flavor of Wisconsin*. Madison: Wisconsin Historical Society Press, 2009.

Hale, Sarah Josepha. *Early American Cookery: "The Good Housekeeper," 1841*. Mineola, NY: Dover Publications Inc., 1996.

Hedrick, U. P. *A History of Horticulture in America to 1860*. Portland, OR: Timber Press, 1988.

Henderson, Peter. *Garden and Farm Topics*. New York: Peter Henderson & Co., 1884.

XCVIII

Opposite page:
A photograph of Alex Smith's farm in Bear Creek near Lone Rock provides a rare view of a Wisconsin farm's kitchen garden, seen to the right of the house, circa 1875.
WHI IMAGE ID 4886

The Michael Baltus family in Wood County displays a selection of fresh garden produce, circa 1895. Behind them, their new frame house towers above their earlier cabin-style home.
WHI IMAGE ID 1793

Henderson, Peter. *Gardening for Pleasure*. New York: Orange Judd Company, 1887.

Henderson, Peter. *Gardening for Profit*. New York: Orange Judd Company, 1867.

Henderson, Peter. *Practical Floriculture*. New York: Orange Judd Company, 1883.

Hill, May Brawley. *Grandmother's Garden: The Old-Fashioned American Garden, 1865–1915*. New York: Harry N. Abrams Inc., 1995.

The Illustrated Annual Register of Rural Affairs for 1858, no. 4. Albany, NY: Luther Tucker & Son, 1858.

Illustrated Catalogue of American Hardware of the Russell and Erwin Manufacturing Co. New Britain, CT: Russell and Erwin Manufacturing Company, 1865.

Johnson, Allen F. "The Wesley P. Benson House: A Vermont-Yankee Craftsman's Household in the Village of Fort Atkinson, Jefferson County, Wisconsin." Old World Wisconsin unpublished manuscript, August 13, 1982.

Johnson, Mrs. S. O. *Every Woman Her Own Flower Gardener*. New York: Henry T. Williams, 1875.

Kent, Elizabeth. *Flora Domestica, or The Portable Flower-Garden*. London: Taylor and Hessey, 1825.

The Ladies' Floral Cabinet and Pictorial Home Companion. New York: Henry T. Williams, 1874, 1875, 1876, 1877.

Leighton, Ann. *American Gardens in the Eighteenth Century*. Amherst: The University of Massachusetts Press, 1986.

Leighton, Ann. *American Gardens of the Nineteenth Century*. Amherst: The University of Massachusetts Press, 1987.

Pape, Alan. "A Taste for Rural Embellishment. A Plan for the Landscaping of the James Harvey Sanford Farm Exhibit of 1860 at Old World Wisconsin." Old World Wisconsin unpublished manuscript, February 16, 1983.

Perkins. Martin C. "A Proposal for the Acquisition of the J. H. Sanford House, Town of LaGrange, Walworth County." Old World Wisconsin unpublished manuscript, December 4, 1981.

Quest-Ritson, Charles. *The English Garden. A Social History*. Boston: David R. Godine, 2003.

Quinn. P. T. *Money in the Garden*. New York: Orange Judd Company, 1871.

Rand, Edward Sprague, Jr. *Flowers for the Parlor and Garden*. Boston: J. E. Tilton & Company, 1868.

Rand, Edward Sprague, Jr. *Garden Flowers: How to Cultivate Them*. Boston: J. E. Tilton & Company, 1866.

R. H. Allen & Co. 1871 Retail Priced Catalogue of Garden and Field Seeds & Grains. New York: R. H. Allen & Co., 1871.

Transactions of the Wisconsin State Horticultural Society, vol. 16. Madison: Democrat Printing Company, 1886.

Vick's Flower and Vegetable Garden. Rochester, NY: James Vick, 1876, 1878, [1880?], 1882.

Vick's Illustrated Monthly Magazine. Rochester, NY: James Vick, 1878–1890.

Watson, Alexander. *The American Home Garden*. New York: Harper and Brothers, 1859.

Williams, Henry T. *Window Gardening*. New York: Henry T. Williams, 1876.

Wisconsin & Iowa Farmer, and Northwestern Cultivator, vol. 3. Racine, WI: Mark Miller, 1851.

Wisconsin & Iowa Farmer, and Northwestern Cultivator, vol. 5. Janesville, WI: Mark Miller, 1853.

Wisconsin & Iowa Farmer, and Northwestern Cultivator, vol. 6. Janesville, WI: Mark Miller and S. P. Lathrop, 1854.

Wisconsin & Iowa Farmer, and Northwestern Cultivator, vol. 7. Janesville, WI: Mark Miller and S. P. Lathrop, 1855.

Wisconsin Farmers' Institutes: A Hand-Book of Agriculture, no. 10. Milwaukee: The Evening Wisconsin Co., 1896.

GERMANS

Bayard, Tania. *Sweet Herbs and Sundry Flowers: Medieval Gardens and the Gardens of the Cloisters*. New York: The Metropolitan Museum of Art; Boston: David R. Godine, 1985.

"Documents: Christian Traugott Ficker's Advice to Emigrants." *Wisconsin Magazine of History* 25, no. 2 (December 1941).

The History of Washington and Ozaukee Counties, Wisconsin. Chicago: Western Historical Company, 1881.

Kamphoefner, Walter D., Wolfgang Helbich, and Ulrike Sommer, eds. *News from the Land of Freedom: German Immigrants Write Home*. Ithaca, NY, and London: Cornell University Press, 1991.

Knipping, Mark. "A Pomeranian Wheat Farm of Dodge County, Wisconsin (ca. 1860)." Old World Wisconsin unpublished manuscript, February 1, 1977.

Long, Amos, Jr., *The Pennsylvania German Family Farm*. Breinigsville, PA: The Pennsylvania German Society, 1972.

Miller, James William. "German Heirloom Gardening Research Report." Old World Wisconsin unpublished manuscript, February 2002.

Oberle, Korinne. "Schulz Farm Interpretive Plan." Old World Wisconsin unpublished manuscript, 1977.

Perkins, Martin C. "The Friedrich Koepsell Farm: A Pomeranian Carpenter's Farmstead of Washington County (ca. 1880)." Old World Wisconsin unpublished manuscript, August 31, 1978.

Renn, Erin McCawley. "Early 19th Century German Immigrants Gardens." *Midwest Open Air Museums Magazine* 12 (1991).

Stark, Judith. "Plant Materials Used by Pomeranian Immigrants in Wisconsin During the Nineteenth Century." Old World Wisconsin unpublished manuscript, April 16, 1974.

Zeitlin, Richard H. *Germans in Wisconsin*. Madison: The State Historical Society of Wisconsin, 2000.

NORWEGIANS

Blegen, Theodore C. *Norwegian Migration to America: The American Transition*. Northfield, MN: Norwegian-American Historical Association, 1940.

Bühler, Karl-Dietrich. *The Scandinavian Garden*. London: Frances Lincoln Limited, 2000.

A Chronicle of Old Muskego: The Diary of Søren Bache, 1839–1847. Northfield, MN: Norwegian-American Historical Association, 1951.

A Chronicler of Immigrant Life: Svein Nilsson's Articles in Billed-Magazin, *1868–1870*. Northfield, MN: Norwegian-American Historical Association, 1982.

Marinette, 1895: bounty of the garden!
WHI IMAGE ID 1979

Fapso, Richard J. *Norwegians in Wisconsin*. Madison: The State Historical Society of Wisconsin, 1977.

Fapso, Richard J. *Norwegians in Wisconsin*. Madison: Wisconsin Historical Society Press, 2001.

Fapso, Richard J., and Mark H. Knipping. "The Knud Crispinusen Fossebrekke House: A Norwegian Settler's Cabin in the Woods, ca. 1845." Old World Wisconsin unpublished manuscript, June 30, 1978.

Gjerde, Jon. *From Peasants to Farmers: The Migration from Balestrand, Norway, to the Upper Middle West*. New York: Cambridge University Press, 1985.

Gjerde, Jon. *The Minds of the West: Ethnocultural Evolution in the Rural Middle West, 1830–1917*. Chapel Hill: The University of North Carolina Press, 1997.

Hale, Frederick. *Swedes in Wisconsin*. Madison: Wisconsin Historical Society Press, 2002.

Ibarra, Robert Antonio. "Ethnicity Genuine and Spurious: A Study of a Norwegian Community in Rural Wisconsin." PhD diss., University of Wisconsin–Madison, 1976.

Knipping, Mark H., and Richard J. Fapso. "The Anders Ellingsen Kvaale Farm: Early Norwegian Commercial Agriculture, circa 1865." Old World Wisconsin unpublished manuscript, January 16, 1978.

Koren, Elisabeth. *The Diary of Elisabeth Koren, 1853–1855*. Translated and edited by David T. Nelson. Northfield, MN: Norwegian-American Historical Association, 1955.

Kroemer, Thomas, and Astrid Pfeifer. "The Anders Kvaale Farmstead Exhibit Interpretive Manual." Old World Wisconsin unpublished manuscript, March 20, 2001.

Standing in his five-acre field of cabbage in Grantsburg, Martin Anderson proudly displays a prizewinner, circa 1895.
WHI IMAGE ID 1982

Miller, Margaret M., and Sigmund Aarseth. *Norwegian Rosemaling: Decorative Painting on Wood*. New York: Charles Scribner's Sons, 1974.

Stokker, Kathleen. *Remedies and Rituals: Folk Medicine in Norway and the New Land*. St. Paul: Minnesota Historical Society Press, 2007.

Weatherford, Doris. *Foreign and Female: Immigrant Women in America, 1840–1930*. New York: Facts on File Inc., 1995.

IRISH

Diner, Hasia R. *Erin's Daughters in America: Irish Immigrant Women in the Nineteenth Century*. Baltimore: The Johns Hopkins University Press, 1983.

Evans, E. Estyn. *Irish Folk Ways*. New York: The Devin-Adair Company, 1957.

Holmes, David G. *Irish in Wisconsin*. Madison: Wisconsin Historical Society Press, 2004.

Holmes, Fred L. *Old World Wisconsin: Around Europe in the Badger State*. Eau Claire, WI: E. M. Hale and Company, 1944.

Johnson, Allen F. "The Mary Hafford House: An Irish Widow's Household in the Village of Hubbleton, Jefferson County, Wisconsin." Old World Wisconsin unpublished manuscript, January 20, 1982.

Logan, Patrick. *Irish Country Cures*. New York: Sterling Publishing Co. Inc., 1994.

Miller, Kirby A. *Emigrants and Exiles: Ireland and the Irish Exodus to North America*. New York: Oxford University Press, 1985.

Mulrooney, Margaret M. *Black Powder, White Lace: The du Pont Irish and Cultural Identity in Nineteenth-Century America*. Hanover, NH, and London: University Press of New England, 2002.

Reeves-Smyth, Terence. *The Garden Lover's Guide to Ireland*. New York: Princeton Architectural Press, 2001.

Robinson, William. *The English Flower Garden*. New York: The Amaryllis Press, 1984.

Weatherford, Doris. *Foreign and Female: Immigrant Women in America, 1840–1930*. New York: Facts on File Inc., 1995.

DANES

Bühler, Karl-Dietrich. *The Scandinavian Garden*. London: Frances Lincoln Limited, 2000.

Hale, Frederick. *Danes in Wisconsin*. Madison: Wisconsin Historical Society Press, 2005.

Holmes, Fred L. *Old World Wisconsin: Around Europe in the Badger State*. Eau Claire, WI: E. M. Hale and Company, 1944.

Hvidt, Kristian. *Flugten til Amerika eller Drivkraefter i masseudvandringen fra Danmark 1868–1914*. Copenhagen: Universitetsforlaget i Aarhus, 1971.

Jeppesen, Torben Grøngaard. *Dannebrog on the American Prairie. A Danish Colony Project in the 1870s—Land Purchase and the Beginnings of a Town*. Translated by James D. Iversen. Odense, Denmark: Odense City Museums, 2000.

Knipping, Mark H. "The Kristen Pedersen Farm: A Danish Dairy Farm of Polk County, Wisconsin, circa 1890." Old World Wisconsin unpublished manuscript, September 26, 1980.

Pedersen, Ellen Johansen. "As I Remember . . ." Typewritten copy in Old World Wisconsin files, circa 1975.

Toman, Rolf, ed. *European Garden Design from Classical Antiquity to the Present Day*. Bonn, Germany: Tandem Verlag GmbH, 2007.

POLES

Buist, Robert. *The Family Kitchen Gardener*. New York: A. O. Moore, Agricultural Book Publisher, 1858.

Dembińska, Maria. *Food and Drink in Medieval Poland*. Translated by Magdalena Thomas. Revised and adapted by William Woys Weaver. Philadelphia: University of Pennsylvania Press, 1999.

Goc, Michael J. *Native Realm: The Polish-American Community of Portage County 1857–1992*. Stevens Point and Friendship, WI: Worzalla Publishing and New Past Press Inc., 1992.

Knab, Sophie Hodorowicz. *Polish Herbs, Flowers & Folk Medicine*. New York: Hippocrene Books Inc., 1999.

"Kruza House Interpretive Plan." Old World Wisconsin unpublished manuscript, 1989.

Mikos, Susan G. "Folkways of Polish Immigrants." Old World Wisconsin unpublished manuscript, March 22, 1999.

Price, Susan Davis. *Growing Home: Stories of Ethnic Gardening*. Minneapolis: University of Minnesota Press, 2000.

Sandberg, Neil C. *Ethnic Identity and Assimilation: The Polish-American Community*. New York: Praeger Publishers, 1974.

Weatherford, Doris. *Foreign and Female: Immigrant Women in America, 1840–1930*. New York: Facts on File Inc., 1995.

FINNS

Bühler, Karl-Dietrich. *The Scandinavian Garden*. London: Frances Lincoln Limited, 2000.

Holmes, Fred L. *Old World Wisconsin: Around Europe in the Badger State*. Eau Claire, WI: E. M. Hale and Company, 1944.

Knipping, Mark H. *Finns in Wisconsin*. Madison: Wisconsin Historical Society Press, 2008.

Knipping, Mark H., and Richard H. Zeitlin. "The Heikki Ketola Farm: A Finnish Dairy Farm in Bayfield County, circa 1915." Old World Wisconsin unpublished manuscript, April 15, 1978.

Knipping, Mark H., Richard H. Zeitlin, and Peter D. Frank. "The Jacob Rankinen Farm: A Finnish Homestead in the Cutover, circa 1897." Old World Wisconsin unpublished manuscript, March 24, 1978.

Ojakangas, Beatrice A. *The Finnish Cookbook*. New York: Crown Publishers Inc., 1964.

Price, Susan Davis. *Growing Home: Stories of Ethnic Gardening*. Minneapolis: University of Minnesota Press, 2000.

Wisconsin Farmers' Institutes: A Hand-Book of Agriculture, no. 10. Milwaukee: The Evening Wisconsin Co., 1896.

Wisconsin Farmers' Institutes: A Hand-Book of Agriculture, no. 17. Madison: Wisconsin Farmers' Institutes, 1903.

Wisconsin Farmers' Institutes: A Hand-Book of Agriculture, no. 20. Madison: Wisconsin Farmers' Institutes, 1906.

Index

Page locators in *italics* indicate photographs and drawings; **bold** index entries indicate recipe titles.